The POINT of No Return

Tackling Your Next New Assignment With
COURAGE & COMMON SENSE

RICK RENNER

Harrison House
Tulsa, OK

The Point of No Return:
Tackling Your Next New Assignment
With Courage and Common Sense
ISBN 978-160683-531-9
Copyright © 1993 by
Rick Renner Ministries, Inc.

Published by Harrison House Pubishers
Tulsa, Ok 74145
In partnership with Institute Books, Inc.
Tulsa, Ok 74133
Paperback Edition 2014

Editorial Consultants: Cynthia Hansen and Andrell Corbin
Text Design: Lisa Simpson, www.SimpsonProductions.net
Graphic Design: Debbie Pullman, www.ZoeLifeCreative.com

DEDICATION

To Dr. William Bennett, one of the greatest men God has ever allowed me to know, to serve, and to claim as a friend. I am so grateful for all the wonderful things you taught me and imparted to my life as I served alongside you in the earlier years of my life. Thank you for teaching me, instructing me, correcting me, and giving me a godly example to follow throughout the course of my life and ministry. Most of all, thank you for teaching me to always give the glory to Jesus. As you always exhorted me in the many letters you've written to me over the years: *Soli Deo Gloria.*

CONTENTS

PREFACE

The term "the point of no return" is a navigational term that can be illustrated by the following example: When Charles Lindbergh flew across the Atlantic Ocean for the first time, there came a moment in his trip when it was impossible for him to return home to America; he had only enough fuel left to continue on toward Europe. Lindbergh had reached the point of no return.

The point of no return will most often contain the elements of *risk*, *striking out into unknown territory*, and *accomplishing what looks impossible*. For a wide variety of reasons, not many people ever experience what it's like to step out and conquer the challenge of such a moment.

As Christians, however, we should experience these strategic moments not just once, but *whenever* it's time for God to give us our next assignment. We may have expended years of prayer, faith, and hard work, believing for a dream the Lord has put in our hearts to come to pass. Then one day the opportunity for that dream to be fulfilled lands on our doorstep, and at that moment, we reach the point of no return. We've invested too much in God's plan for our lives and grown too much in our knowledge of Him to turn back or disobey. We *must* go forward, because to turn back would mean the ultimate nullification of our divine purpose.

There is no doubt in my mind that my family and I are right in the middle of a tremendous miracle of God. We have passed the point of no return again and again to get where we are today, and we are passing another point of no return as we get ready to fulfill the next phase of God's call on our lives.

When I first wrote this book in 1993, our family had just moved to the USSR a couple of years earlier to begin the adventure of a lifetime. In our office in that part of the world, there was a huge map of the USSR with big, red circles that our staff had drawn to indicate all the regions where we wanted to broadcast God's Word on television to what had become the *former* Soviet Union soon after our arrival. Although Denise and I were told that this dream was impossible, we knew God had spoken to our hearts, and we set out to do what He had asked us to do. As I prepare to release this new edition of *The Point of No Return*, we've now been pursuing this divine adventure for more than two decades without interruption.

When we took those first steps of faith, we didn't realize our TV outreach was going to become one of the largest instruments for the Gospel in this part of the world. And God didn't have only a TV ministry in mind. His future plan for us included starting multiple churches, constructing major church facilities, providing oversight for several hundred churches, developing outreaches for the poor and needy, and supporting a host of missionaries ministering throughout the former USSR and around the world.

When we first started this season of ministry on the other side of the world, we didn't know that these wonderful developments would follow. We've discovered over these years of walking with God that as we obey Him, He keeps giving us greater challenges. However, He also keeps leading us into ever-greater victories — because *anything* is possible through Christ!

I'm so glad we didn't listen to the negative voices who said that all of this was impossible and that we shouldn't attempt it! Had we heeded them, we would have missed all the wonderful things God wanted to do in and through our lives.

As I grow in my own Christian experience and walk with the Lord, I find myself taking a more and more practical approach to finding the will of God and doing it. Denise and I and our ministry team are doing what others would call crazy, impossible, and even insane — but it's working!

We've discovered that doing the "impossible" isn't impossible at all as long as we seek God's wisdom to understand what steps to take, how to proceed, and, just as importantly, how quickly we should move ahead. If we've discerned the Holy Spirit's answers to these questions — and if we've built a strong spiritual foundation for our lives — we can do anything God asks us to do, no matter how difficult it looks to the natural eye.

Do you sense God's challenge in your heart to become more effective in pursuing His plan for your life? Is your heart saying, "I'm ready to do whatever God wants me to do with my life"? If so, this book will speak directly to *you*. Whether you're a student, businessperson, minister, teenager, parent, husband, or wife — you will benefit from reading this commonsense approach to taking on your next divine assignment.

This book is for people who are ready to move beyond the status quo and accomplish something significant with their lives. It is for people who know that God is calling them to move up higher; to go faster and further than they ever have before in their walk with Him; and to pass beyond the point of no return — that place from which there is no turning back from obeying the Lord.

It's my prayer that after you are finished reading this book, you will never again be content to stay the way you are. I pray that you will rise up in faith, accept God's next impossible task for your life, and boldly move forward into previously unknown territory. Only then will you discover the fullness of God's favor, blessing, and miraculous power!

If I have just described you, welcome to a life of faith and adventure! Every aspect of your life is about to change. Get ready to encounter your own personal "point of no return"!

Rick Renner
Moscow, Russia, 2012

Now after the death of Moses the servant of the Lord it came to pass, that the Lord spake unto Joshua the son of Nun, Moses' minister, saying, Moses my servant is dead; now therefore arise, go over this Jordan, thou, and all this people, unto the land which I do give to them, even to the children of Israel.

Every place that the sole of your foot shall tread upon, that have I given unto you, as I said unto Moses. From the wilderness and this Lebanon even unto the great river, the river Euphrates, all the land of the Hittites, and unto the great sea toward the going down of the sun, shall be your coast.

There shall not any man be able to stand before thee all the days of thy life: as I was with Moses, so I will be with thee: I will not fail thee, nor forsake thee. Be strong and of a good courage: for unto this people shalt thou divide for an inheritance the land, which I sware unto their fathers to give them. Only be thou strong and very courageous, that thou mayest observe to do according to all the law, which Moses my servant commanded thee: turn not from it to the right hand or to the left, that thou mayest prosper whithersoever thou goest.

This book of the law shall not depart out of thy mouth; but thou shalt meditate therein day and night, that thou mayest observe to do according to all that is written therein: for then thou shalt make thy way prosperous, and then thou shalt have good success.

Have not I commanded thee? Be strong and of a good courage; be not afraid, neither be thou dismayed: for the Lord thy God is with thee whithersoever thou goest.

Joshua 1:1-9

CHAPTER ONE

THE POINT OF NO RETURN

Have you ever fervently prayed and earnestly longed for a God-given dream in your heart that finally came to pass? If you're like me, every cell and fiber of your being waited in anticipation to receive the answer to your prayer — and then suddenly, it happened! Things began moving so quickly that you felt like your head was swimming!

Stepping out in faith to accomplish something new and adventuresome that God has asked you to do — something you've never done before — can be scary. The reason it's scary is *not* because you're certain that you'll fail or that God will prove unfaithful to help you. It's daunting simply because you've never done anything like it before. The prospect of entering into unknown territory can make you feel a little shaky on the inside.

As you approach the moment when you know you can't turn back — that instant in time when you realize the past is gone and your only option is to press ahead to do the will of God — you probably feel conflicting emotions, like an earthquake in the pit of your stomach. After all the years of praying for this moment to come, it's finally here! Reality is striking hard and fast. You wish you could turn back the clock and think about it for just a few more days, but that is no longer an option.

Your time to step out in faith has finally come.

The days when you could get away with passing off your responsibilities to someone else are gone. No longer can you back up, slow down, give the lead to someone else, or just say, "I'll do it later." Yesterday's luxury of saying, "Someday..." is now a memory from the past. The time of delaying the inevitable is over.

> Yesterday's luxury of saying, "Someday..." is now a memory from the past. The time of delaying the inevitable is over.

You have reached the point of no return!

There are many times in people's lives when they face the point of no return. Some of these occasions are small and seemingly insignificant, such as a person taking his first dive off a diving board or making his first entrance in a school play. Other landmark moments are far greater in scope, such as resigning from a secure position with a large corporation to start a business or having one's first baby.

Each time I've personally faced the point of no return, whether it was large or small, a complex mix of overwhelming feelings has welled up from deep within me — including excitement, anxiety, and a sense of eternal destiny. These feelings arise in all of us whenever we step out in faith to obey God. We're moving beyond what is familiar and comfortable into the unknown, just as Peter stepped out of the boat onto the raging sea to walk toward Jesus (*see* Matthew 14:25-29).

Although the small steps forward in our lives may seem insignificant at the time, they are necessary and vital to the fulfillment of our God-given dreams. I honestly believe that it would have been very difficult, if not impossible, to take the incredible leaps of faith the Holy Spirit has required of me in recent years if I hadn't chosen to take smaller steps into the unknown in my earlier years. The Bible says we should not take lightly our small beginnings, and I am one servant of the Lord who takes that divine admonition seriously. I have a great respect for my small beginnings.

All of my early choices to trust God over my own natural reasoning and preferences built my faith so that later I could begin trusting Him in situations that would affect not only me, but also those around me. And over the course of many years spent walking with the Lord, I've learned this crucial lesson: *When God calls you beyond the point of no return, He has a plan waiting for you that far exceeds your wildest imagination.*

MY OWN EXPERIENCE
WITH THE POINT OF NO RETURN

Many years ago when Denise and I were newly married, we were pastoring a very small church in Arkansas — a church I'd started on my own that *wasn't* a part of God's will for our lives. After two difficult years, God spoke to me and said that He wanted us to abandon what He had never asked us to do and move into the next phase of His plan for our lives. I remember how I felt when I told Denise that we were resigning from our church, without any knowledge of where we were supposed to go or what we were supposed to do. Some of our family members — and, at times, even Denise and I — thought we had lost our minds for undertaking such a huge leap of faith.

Our church was small, and our income was very low. Nevertheless, we had a house (albeit a very old one) and friends who lived around us. Stepping out in faith to resign from that church was a monumental undertaking for us, but we knew God was changing the course of our lives to get us back on track and move us forward in His perfect plan.

As I stood in front of our little congregation and told them we were resigning, my stomach churned. I realized that once our announcement was made, there was no turning back. *This was the point of no return in our lives.*

After our resignation, Denise and I spent 30 days praying and waiting on the Lord until our spirits were able to discern His direction for our lives and ministry. The Holy Spirit took me back to the vision He had originally given me years before. He tenderly spoke to my heart, *"I've called you to teach the Word of God to My people. I want you to take your ministry to believers across the nation."*

When I first heard those words, I was *petrified* at the thought of launching out into this new, unknown territory. I knew I had a gift to teach God's Word, but I'd never taught outside of our little circle. This new assignment God had just given me sounded as big as Goliath must have looked to little David!

To begin with, who knew us? We had been living in a small town in Arkansas for five years, and we weren't well known. Living in that little town didn't exactly put us in the mainstream of American life, so we were unfamiliar to most people outside of our tiny circle — and I do mean *tiny*!

When I stood in front of our family and told them that our next step in life was to begin a nationwide teaching ministry, their response was certainly logical. "How in the world are you going to do that when no one knows who you are?" they asked. "How will you support yourself as you get started? Do you have any idea how to do what you're talking about?"

I had the same answer to all of my family's questions: "I don't know!" But their questions didn't bother me because they were voicing the same questions I was privately asking myself! All I knew was that the Holy Spirit had spoken to my heart and was preparing us for a new adventure. When He spoke to me and I said, "Yes, Lord," faith was imparted, and I was ready to carry out His plan for my life. I was excited, scared, thrilled, petrified, happy, and shaken to the core — all at once!

Stepping out into an entirely new realm was exciting and scary. The truth is, I was asking even more questions than my family and friends had asked me — questions such as:

- "What is the first step we should take to begin a nation-wide teaching ministry?"

- "How do people become familiar with us so they will know to invite us to their churches?"

- "What if we take this step of faith and then absolutely no one wants us to minister the Word of God in his church?"

- "How will I feed my family and pay our bills until our teaching ministry gets established?"

Anyone who steps out into uncharted territory in order to obey God asks these kinds of questions. Denise and I were called to take our teaching ministry to the nation and the world, but businessmen ask the same kinds of questions when they launch out into a realm of business they have never before attempted. Regardless of the new assignment or calling a person is pursuing, he will ask these kinds of questions if he wants to succeed in the endeavor.

As we took our first steps of faith to obey God in this new assignment, I felt an earthquake of emotions in the pit of my stomach. We were doing what God wanted us to do, but because it was new, we naturally felt the shaky feeling that people experience when they step into brand-new, uncharted territory.

All Denise and I knew was that we had received a word from God to start this new season in our lives. Certain that God had spoken to us, we commenced on our new pilgrimage of faith — an adventure in Him that has reaped incredible supernatural fruit ever since. In fact, since we passed that point of no return, several million books have been printed and sold, thousands of audio and video teachings have been distributed, and Denise and I have ministered the Word in thousands of churches, seminars, and meetings around the world.

Most significantly, our acting on that word from the Lord to start an itinerant teaching ministry prepared us for the next major step of faith that God would require of us seven years later — *moving to the former bastion of Communism once known as the Soviet Union.* That new assignment was definitely *not* a part of my plans, but by then I had learned my lesson: It's far better to obey God than to do things my way!

The Ministry Expands to the USSR

The first years of our teaching ministry were not always easy as we struggled to make ends meet. But several years later, Denise and I were traveling all over the world ministering the Word of God. By that time, we'd seen God do many miraculous things with our lives. I had gained a good reputation in the United States as a teacher and an author and had preached in literally thousands of meetings. The lean times were coming to an end, and we were receiving approximately 900 invitations each year to speak in some of the nation's greatest churches.

We bought the house of our dreams; our staff in the Tulsa office was as committed to our ministry as we were; and my books, tapes, and videos were being distributed by the hundreds of thousands. The ministry was fulfilling a need in the Body of

Christ, which was very gratifying, and God was blessing us personally beyond our wildest dreams. Everything was perfect in our lives, and we were enjoying every minute of it.

Then God spoke.

While I was on a mission trip to what was at that time the Soviet Union, the Holy Spirit spoke to my heart about His next assignment for us. He said, "Because of all the people who are being saved in the USSR right now, I am calling you and your family to live here and teach the Bible to believers. They need to be established in the foundational truths of My Word."

I nearly fell over when the Lord said that to me! Astonished, I asked the Lord for further clarification. He spoke to my heart once again, saying that because of the outpouring of His Spirit upon the USSR, the need for good teachers was imperative and immediate.

I understood that in such a time as this — when possibly the largest door for the Gospel in more than 1,000 years had swung wide open — balanced and experienced teachers of the Bible were undeniable necessities in the USSR. The masses of new believers needed help building a solid foundation of truth in their lives.

However, I was still stunned and somewhat aghast by the thought of leaving everything behind. I prayed, "Lord, have You forgotten what we're doing in the United States? Do You remember that You called us to teach the Word in America? Maybe You overlooked the fact that we have an office staff in Tulsa who need to be paid every month. And have You forgotten that I don't even like missions?" But at the core of it all, my real fear was not leaving America or moving to the mission field — I would do whatever God required of me. My real fear was the financial challenge of the assignment.

I kept thinking, *How am I going to support a ministry in the United States if we live in the Soviet Union and never have any meetings in the States? Will our partners forget about us and stop contributing to our ministry? Will I be able to pay our bills? How am I going to pay the salaries of our staff in the Tulsa office if I'm living on the other side of the world?*

Nevertheless, God's firm voice kept whispering to me, *"This is the next step in My plan for your life. If you'll obey Me, I'll make sure you are covered financially."*

> God's firm voice kept whispering to me, *"This is the next step in My plan for your life. If you'll obey Me, I'll make sure you are covered financially."*

This was a great test for me. I was comfortable in my present ministry, and I was happy and proud of our new house in Tulsa. I was enjoying a measure of notoriety among believers and ministers in the Church whom I had admired and respected for years. But God was asking me to put all those things aside and follow Him into unknown territory yet again. So I swallowed hard and accepted the fact that it was time for another big step of faith.

Sitting on the couch in our family room, Denise and I talked and prayed about this huge change in the direction of our lives. We were both American to the bone and proud of it! We had been raised in the era when the Soviet Union was our big enemy. In fact, we could both remember being taught in grade school how to protect ourselves in the case of a nuclear fallout! We could recall being rushed down hallways and stairs into the basements of our schools during practice drills to protect ourselves from a military onslaught of Communism.

As Americans, we were sure there was no better nation in the world than the United States of America — and, naturally, the thought of moving to a country that had historically persecuted

Christians didn't sound appealing to us, especially since we had three young sons! But as we prayed together that day, we both knew in our hearts that God was truly calling our family to move to the USSR.

As Denise and I worked through our fears and recognized that this was God's will for our lives, a flood of faith and excitement began to pour into our souls. We were thrilled just to think that we would be teaching the Bible in a place where the people had known nothing but atheistic Communism. Only God could do such a marvelous thing!

Our fears turned to faith as we rec-ognized the hand of God on our lives to prepare us for this new season. The real-ization that we were going to be a part of a major outpouring of His Spirit in the last days began to sink into our hearts. We became supernaturally filled with courage to begin our new adventure!

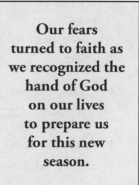

Our fears turned to faith as we recognized the hand of God on our lives to prepare us for this new season.

I called our families and staff and gave them the news. They were shocked, but the same grace that rested upon us came upon them. They took the news like troopers and asked what they could do to help us make this major transi-tion in our lives. Then I called our pastor and talked with him about our decision. He replied without hesitation, "This is God's plan for your life."

Everything was moving ahead peaceably and nicely — and then I knew it was time to make the first public announcement about our big move. I was at an out-of-town meeting, excited to stand in front of that crowd and make the announcement. The leaders of the church came forward and laid hands on me, prophesying about how God would use my family in the Soviet

Union. My adrenaline was flowing, and my emotions were at an all-time high!

After the meeting, I went back to my hotel room and called Denise to tell her that I'd made the big announcement. However, after I hung up the phone and sat down in my hotel room — *all alone* — the reality of what I'd just announced began to hit me like a semi-truck. Every ounce of fear that had been hiding in my soul over the years suddenly decided to pay me a visit, and my mind was flooded with questions.

- *What have you done?*

- *Why did you make such a stupid announcement to all those people?*

- *What if your partners stop supporting you because they don't see you as often?*

- *What if the Communists begin to persecute believers again, and your family is caught in the middle of a horrible mess?*

- *What if you can't support your family or your headquarters in Tulsa?*

- *WHAT WILL YOU DO?*

Then the devil stepped in to fuel those inner fears, bombarding my mind with more accusing thoughts: *How stupid can you be! If you hadn't publicly announced what God was calling you to do, you could have disobeyed, and no one would have known it but you and God! Now if you don't follow through on your plans, everyone will think that you're spiritually unstable and that you don't really know the voice of God.*

I felt absolutely trapped. Suddenly I understood why the apostle Paul called himself "the prisoner of the Lord" (*see* Ephesians 4:1). Like Paul, I was chained to a new commitment to Jesus

Christ from which there was no recourse. This new commitment to obey the Lord was final and binding.

I began to feel the same earthquake of emotions in the pit of my stomach that I'd felt years earlier when we left our church in Arkansas — and then again when we began our itinerant teaching ministry throughout the United States. Furthermore, the huge inner earthquake I felt that night after making my big announcement had scores of aftershocks that shook me for weeks to come!

It wasn't a lack of faith or distrust in God that created those shaky feelings in me. Rather, I had a profound awareness that God was calling us to do something bigger than ourselves — something that we'd never done before and that we surely could not do without His help. I felt completely and utterly dependent upon Him and fully aware that, without His help, we would fail.

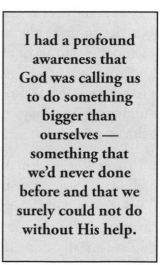

I had a profound awareness that God was calling us to do something bigger than ourselves — something that we'd never done before and that we surely could not do without His help.

Because we're all creatures of habit, it can be a real challenge when God asks us to step out in faith and do something new. Our comfortable little world gets shaken as He calls us to expand our vision — and that nearly always creates temporary feelings of uneasiness and discomfort. Thank God, those emotions eventually pass as we follow Him. I personally believe that one of the main reasons God calls us again and again to the point of no return is to remind us that He is our total Source of security, that nothing is impossible with Him, and that we can do all things through Him.

THAT ISN'T THE END OF THE STORY!

Denise and I began to seek the guidance of the Holy Spirit to answer all of our questions. The first place we were to call "home" in what would soon become the *former* Soviet Union was a small town called Jelgava in Latvia, a Baltic republic of the USSR. Within months of our arrival, Latvia would regain its status as an independent nation, but when we made the decision to move, it was still a part of the USSR. Prior to moving, we began to work out the best means of communication between Latvia and our U.S. office. We even developed an emergency plan in the event that our family was caught in the middle of a political crisis.

We scrimped, saved, and used our money as wisely as possible in order to make the move without burdening our ministry and partners. We found a buyer for our dream house, put most of our furniture in storage or gave it away, donated our ministry van to a missionary in Mexico, sold our family station wagon, and broke the news to our boys that we had to find another home for our beloved family dog.

After a year of making preparations, packing a multitude of boxes, and going through our tearful goodbyes with family and friends, we finally boarded the first of several airplanes that would carry us across the globe to our new home. Our hearts rejoiced that we'd really done it! We had put aside our doubts, fears, and creature comforts, and we had obeyed the word of the Lord. A major milestone in our lives had been passed!

STRETCHING AND GROWING
BY LEAPS AND BOUNDS

We officially moved in 1991 just as the Soviet Union was collapsing. By early 1992, Denise and I and our sons were beginning to feel at home in a very new environment — truly a work of divine grace that we acclimated so quickly to this new and different world where God had sent us.

After arriving in Jelgava, we settled into our new home in no time at all. We began teaching the Word of God in a local Bible school and preaching in churches all around our region. Our boys quickly started picking up the language, relishing every hardship along the way. To them, shoveling coal to keep the house warm or boiling water to take a warm bath was the greatest fun they'd ever had. God even blessed them with a new dog!

News of Denise's beautiful operatic voice traveled quickly as well, and she was invited to sing at a conservatory of music in the city of Riga, the capital city of Latvia. After Denise sang and testified of Jesus, we stood in awe as we witnessed many tearful, hard-line Communists receive Christ as their Lord and Savior.

Not only were we enjoying ourselves and truly feeling at home, but to our pleasant surprise, we also developed a marvelous and miraculous love for the people there. We had expected adventure and challenge, but the joy of ministering to these precious people — and the deep love we felt for them from the moment we stepped onto Latvian soil — was an awesome extra reward.

The nation we called our new home had been painfully and cruelly oppressed for more than 70 years. Yet right before our eyes, we were seeing miracles in the lives of people who had lived under that spiritual, mental, emotional, and even physical oppression as they began to be wonderfully transformed, healed, and set free by the power of God and His Word!

Realizing that we could have missed all of these tremendous blessings from the Lord, we breathed a sigh of relief that we had obeyed Him in this big leap of faith. We had chosen once again to pass the point of no return, following the Holy Spirit's leading all the way to the now-former USSR!

Then amidst all the joy and excitement about our new life, the Holy Spirit spoke to my heart *again*! He told me, *"Now I'm going to tell you more about the reason I moved you to the former Soviet Union. The next part of My plan for your life is for you to begin teaching the Bible on television to the peoples of the former USSR!"*

My mind was shaken at the very thought! Even in America, I had never had the slightest desire to minister on television. Furthermore, I didn't know if I could legally teach the Bible on television in the newly dissolved USSR. The Soviet Union had collapsed so recently that the people in charge of every level of government were still the same people who had run things under the Communist regime. Just two years earlier, I would have been sent to Siberia for even attempting to broadcast a Christian television program. I kept thinking, *Come on, Lord! I've already obeyed You by moving here! That was a big step of faith! And now You're asking me to do this too? At least give me a month or two more to adjust!*

> All of a sudden I knew exactly where I was. I had been there many times before. God was calling us onward and upward, and the clock was ticking.

Then all of a sudden I knew exactly where I was. I had been there many times before. God was calling us onward and upward, and the clock was ticking. We were once again approaching the point of no return. Life was changing again — only this time the change had come sooner than the last. God had allowed us seven years to build our teaching ministry across the United States before He called us to move to Latvia, but He had allowed us only a few months in the former USSR before He began to speak to us about a television ministry.

We knew there were no other options for us if we were going to obey God with our lives. We also knew this meant that our faith had to grow, we had to change, and we could not look back. God's will had been revealed, and we couldn't pass the buck to someone else. The churning in my stomach started again — but I knew we had gone too far in our walk of obedience to stop now!

Still, a television program sounded crazy to me! I didn't know anyone who had attempted to start a television ministry in the former Soviet Union. (As it turned out, we would become the very first to do it!) The doors to this former bastion of Communism had just opened, and the West had only just begun to bring in new ideas and technology. Therefore, I had no one I could turn to and ask, "How does the TV system work in the Soviet Union?"

In actual fact, *no one* knew the answer to this question, not even those who lived there. Because the mass media had been KGB-controlled, the manner in which the public communications system worked had been kept secret. Thus, we had to learn all of it by ourselves as we followed the Holy Spirit's direction — traveling to places where He told us to go and talking with those to whom He led us.

We jumped on airplanes and flew from one end of the former Soviet Union to the other, even traveling to war zones and to areas where no other American had ever set foot. We spoke with television deputies and technicians, visited with powerful former Communist leaders, and began to negotiate contracts for our TV program in the regions the Holy Spirit had put in our hearts.

What Denise and I were attempting to do sounded so insane, in fact, that even our loyal interpreters thought we were a little "over the edge"! Absolutely no one had attempted to do this before. But despite all the voices who told us this endeavor was impossible, we proceeded with the Lord's direction and began broadcasting our Bible teaching program on television.

Establishing a television ministry in the former USSR once seemed like an overwhelming challenge to Denise and me, but after we did it for a while, it grew to feel quite normal. The fears soon left us, and we began operating our TV ministry just as the Holy Spirit had instructed us to. We have learned that as long as He says, "Do this," we can do it!

If you had told me in the years before we moved to that region of the world that Denise and I were going to launch a TV network, I would have laughed out loud and said, "You've got the wrong guy!" Now we know that the impossible really is possible, and that there is nothing more thrilling and satisfying in life than tackling the impossible — and winning. Through this, we have learned that by God's grace and wisdom, we can do the impossible every day, and it can even seem easy and natural!

Today we reach more than 100 million people every week on television, including the most remote and Muslim-dominated regions of the former Soviet Union. And this figure doesn't even include the multiple millions of Russian-speakers that we reach every day around the globe on five different satellites that carry our programs!

OBEDIENCE RELEASES GOD'S POWER IN YOUR LIFE

> **Your life becomes a supernatural life when you obey God.**

Your life becomes a supernatural life when you obey God.

When God calls you to break camp and move your tent to higher, tougher ground — into a new, unfamiliar realm of obedience and faith — at first it seems like a challenging and even a frightening prospect. But once you've conquered those initial fears and established your obedience in that new realm, you're ready to settle into God's ordained place for your life with a higher and deeper level of peace and trust in Him.

Remarkably, as soon as you're settled into that new place, it will probably be time for you to move up to a higher realm once again! And just like the last time, once you've obeyed the Lord and the fear fades, your faith will move up another notch. That means you'll probably be ready to receive *another* new directive from Heaven that will continue to develop you, challenge you, and conform you into the image of Jesus Christ.

Following the Lord's instructions is a never-ending assignment in the life of an obedient believer.

My family and I are still doing what God has commanded us to do. Denise and I were among the first to move to the former USSR; we've stayed longer than anyone else we know of; and we have consistently held fast to the vision God gave us. As a result, we lead a ministry today that is known throughout the former Soviet Union and to Russian-speakers around the world. Our sons are all married to beautiful Russian girls; we have wonderful Russian grandchildren; and they and their families serve alongside us in this God-blessed ministry. What we thought was a short-term mission commitment has become a lifelong adventure in God! We're so grateful for the millions of lives that have been eternally impacted by the ministry God has entrusted to us. And we're thankful for the faithful partners who give to our ministry — who have never abandoned or forgotten about us, who have stayed with us every step of the way, and who are still with us today!

The earthquake of emotions I used to feel in the pit of my stomach is gone, even though Denise and I and our team are working on the biggest assignments God has ever asked of us — steps of faith that would have scared the life out of me when I was younger! Yet we're moving ahead with absolute peace and confidence in our hearts, because we know that God is leading us and He is faithful to bring to pass what He has promised us. After seeing God's faithfulness demonstrated again and again in our lives, we are now absolutely confident that whenever He tells us to step forward by faith, He *will* enable us to finish what He tells us to start.

> After seeing God's faithfulness demonstrated again and again in our lives, we are now absolutely confident that whenever He tells us to step forward by faith, He *will* enable us to finish what He tells us to start.

Through the years, we've also learned that if we continue obeying the Lord, it won't be long before the Holy Spirit puts a new challenge in our hearts. Then we'll leave our present comfort zone to enter into the next God-ordained phase of our lives. *We'll have to face the point of no return again — and we can hardly wait!*

YOU CAN DO MORE THAN YOU'RE DOING RIGHT NOW

The reason I'm spending time talking about my family's story is that I believe that my personal testimony is relevant to the discussion of "the point of no return."

Some areas of knowledge and wisdom in the Word of God must be lived in order for understanding to come. When it comes to being a doer of the Word, there is no substitute for experience. Thus, the following chapters reflect the pouring out of truths from God's Word that I learned from my own personal experience.

I've learned that we can do whatever God asks us to do — and most often, it is *much more* than what we're doing right now. God's plan is to conform us to the image of Jesus Christ as we take our place in fulfilling His purposes. But that only happens as we live each day using our faith, allowing His compassion to work through us to bless others, and living our lives in obedience to His Word. Otherwise, we're not cooperating with God's plan to change us and transform us into powerful Christians who live and act like His Son.

Believe me, friend, you can do much more than you're doing right now. The only thing that stands in your way is the temptation to give in to feelings of insecurity and fear because God has asked you to do something you've never done before. If you choose your doubts and crippling anxieties over faith and trust in God, you will miss the life of adventure He has planned for you. He may not call you to live in the former Soviet Union, start a television ministry, or lead hundreds of churches as we presently do. But the plan God has for your life, your family, your neighborhood, and your business is every bit as significant and potentially exciting!

Our spiritual success isn't measured by what we do, but by whether or not we do exactly what God asks each of us to do.

I'm certain that Noah never dreamed God would use him to preserve the seed of mankind by building a big boat. Abraham was living a comfortable, affluent life in Ur when God called him to journey to an unknown land and establish a new race of people. Moses assuredly never dreamed that he would topple the Egyptian pharaoh and his army and then receive the commandments of God. And I doubt greatly that Elijah relished the thought of confronting the prophets of Baal.

Young Mary, the mother of Jesus, was just an unknown girl who received a word from God and obeyed it — and as a result, she changed the course of history. Because Mary chose to listen and respond to the Lord in faith, her life — and the lives of all of us — were radically altered the moment she boldly declared, "...Be it unto me according to thy word..." (Luke 1:38).

Most of the disciples were just simple, uneducated men before they were called by Jesus. Surely they had no idea that God would use them to shake the very foundations of the Roman Empire and "turn the world upside down" with the Good News of Jesus Christ (*see* Acts 17:6).

Likewise, the apostle Paul was nicely settled into his lifestyle as a high-ranking, religious Jew prior to his conversion. Clearly he had no idea God would call him, utterly change him, and use him as a champion for the faith he once loathed and raged against. Yet because this one man allowed himself to be used in such a mighty way, we are still partaking of the fruit of his revelations even today.

All of these men and women of God did far more than they originally thought they could do. Our great God is a Master at taking seemingly insignificant lives and making them significant. But if any of these great men and women of God had chosen to remain bound by their human limitations, they would never have accomplished any of these things and would have thus missed out on God's purpose for their lives.

> **When God calls us, He also equips, provides, sustains, and empowers us to do more than we think or even imagine we can do.**

What we must always remember is that when God calls us, He also equips, provides, sustains, and empowers us to do more than we think or even imagine we can do.

Have you prayed that God would use you in great and wonderful ways? Have you dreamed of accomplishing something adventuresome, historic, and life-changing in your family, church, neighborhood, business, or nation?

You have the call of God on your life too!

- You may be an Abraham, who charts a walk of faith for others to follow.

- You may be a Joseph, raised up by God to provide financially and materially for the work of God.

- You may be an Elijah, called by God to minister in extremely difficult situations.

- You may be like one of the disciples — not particularly gifted or educated, but filled with God's ability to tackle the impossible and change the world.

- Or you may even be like the apostle Paul, called to move out of your own comfort zone to minister in places where no one else has ever laid a foundation and to bring heavenly revelation to those who are spiritually famished.

Maybe God is calling you to be a better businessman, to push far beyond where you currently are into bigger and broader dreams. Perhaps He is calling you to be a more excellent student, pastor, educator, or worker. Maybe your heart is being tugged to excel as a husband, father, wife, mother, son, or daughter. Or perhaps the desire of your heart is to become wiser and more dedicated to those you love and serve.

Regardless of where you are in life or what you're doing, one thing is certain: You can be more than you are right now.

Your abilities in Jesus Christ are massive, but they will remain unrealized if you don't listen to the voice of God's Spirit and determine to follow His plan for your life. With the power of the

Holy Spirit working in you, an exciting life is in your future. I promise you — no one who truly obeys God is ever bored!

Your time to move ahead is just in front of you. You may be hearing God's voice speaking to you right now as you read this book. Your point of no return may be starting at this very moment!

> **Regardless of where you are in life or what you're doing, one thing is certain: You can be more than you are right now.**

I'm certain that many believers never experience the point of no return, primarily because of the personal cost involved. They may also be frightened by the prospect of having to continuously depend on the miraculous power of God!

Each time I've been called to press past the point of no return in my own life, I've turned to the Bible and found inspiration, wisdom, and courage. Joshua, who is the primary example I'll use in this book, is one of my favorite heroes of the faith. He bravely faced the point of no return when Moses died and it was suddenly his turn to lead the nation of Israel. Joshua followed in the footsteps of a legend, leading an often rebellious and difficult people into the Promised Land. It was a land filled with milk and honey — and deadly giants.

This is where we'll begin in Chapter Two. Make sure you read carefully, and allow the Holy Spirit to speak to your heart about your own life.

An adventure in faith awaits you!

THINK ABOUT IT

When God opens a door of opportunity before you, He also provides sufficient grace to escort you through it. On the other hand, when you presumptuously try to break open a door for yourself, you will quickly discover that ill-timed, forced opportunities are not fruitful.

Think back on doors that you know God opened for you. Now recall past doors you sought to open for yourself in your own strength. What was the difference between those two experiences? Do you see a similarity between either one of those situations and an opportunity you are facing now? It's crucial to learn from past lessons in order to avoid future missteps.

❦

The unknown is always uncomfortable, mainly because you cannot predict or control it. To step forward into unfamiliar territory requires you to walk by faith and not by sight (2 Corinthians 5:7). Without faith, it is impossible to please God (Hebrews 11:6) — but with faith in Him rather than in yourself, you both honor and please the Lord.

What can you do to cooperate with God as He leads you in fulfilling His plan for your life? The answer to that question will most certainly be outside your comfort zone because it will require faith. What type of change do you tend to resist the most? Are there certain thought patterns or emotions you can identify within yourself that emerge when God begins to steer you outside of your comfort zone?

CHAPTER TWO

IT'S TIME TO MOVE AHEAD

*E*very man or woman who has ever seriously served the Lord throughout human history has experienced moments in their lives when they faced a point of no return. Examples of these landmark moments abound in Scripture, but one of the most powerful and detailed examples the Holy Spirit has given us is found in the Old Testament in the life of Joshua.

Joshua served in the shadow of Moses for decades, just waiting for the time when he would become the leader of God's people. Joshua supported Moses through the struggle with Pharaoh in Egypt; he followed Moses across the Red Sea; he traversed the desert with Moses for 40 years in the wilderness; and he stood beside his mentor on countless occasions when trouble arose among the people of Israel.

Finally, after years of hard work and faithful service, Joshua's moment arrived. But what were the qualities of Joshua's character that allowed him to step over the line in faith and pass the point of no return?

A TERRIBLE CRISIS BIRTHS NEW GREATNESS

The book of Joshua begins by saying, "Now after the death of Moses the servant of the Lord it came to pass, that the Lord spake unto Joshua the son of Nun, Moses' minister..." (Joshua 1:1). The writer of Joshua began this book with a grim reminder that a terrible tragedy had happened to Israel: *Moses had died.*

The children of Israel were facing a great crisis. Their venerated and revered spiritual leader was dead, and they didn't know how they could go any further in God without him. And to make matters worse, God had taken the body of Moses and hidden it somewhere in the desert so the Israelites couldn't find it!

One day as I was studying and pondering this story, it occurred to me why God had hidden Moses' dead body from the people of Israel. Had they known of its location, they probably would have built a magnificent tomb over his grave and stopped their walk of faith in order to camp around their dead leader. Instead of reaching the beautiful, fertile land God had promised them, they probably would have built the "City of Moses" and settled for nothing more than a barren desert as their inheritance!

Moses represented a glorious era of God's power, and the Israelites didn't want to see it draw to a close. People often respond in a similar way today. When a great move of the Holy Spirit comes to an end, believers have a difficult time letting go of that past divine move so they can receive the new thing God wants to do in their lives. This is especially true for those who were part of the former era from the very beginning. Rather than move on with the Spirit of God into new and higher realms of glory, these believers often try to preserve their previous experience with God's power. They choose to stay behind and camp on wonderful memories that are ultimately lifeless and powerless — and as a result, they miss out on the next outpouring of God's Spirit.

God had worked great signs and wonders in the wilderness through Moses. He fed millions of people with manna from Heaven, and He supernaturally provided water from a rock when the land was dry. Yet in spite of those miracles, the desert was supposed to be only a temporary dwelling place. God wanted to give the Israelites something far better. He wanted to give His children the Promised Land — a land flowing with milk and honey!

Because God wanted His people to keep moving forward, He hid Moses' dead body so they couldn't find it and build a memorial around it. It was right for the Israelites to remember the miracles that God wrought in the wilderness and to hold the memory of Moses dear in their hearts. But God didn't want them to stop dead in their tracks and miss what He had planned for them in Canaan.

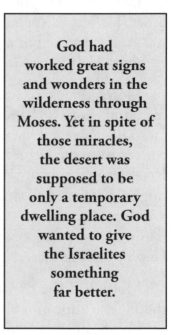

God had worked great signs and wonders in the wilderness through Moses. Yet in spite of those miracles, the desert was supposed to be only a temporary dwelling place. God wanted to give the Israelites something far better.

It must have been psychologically devastating to the Israelites who loved and followed Moses to be unable to lay his body to rest. Physically seeing the body of a loved one in order to say farewell is a natural part of the grieving process. Human nature requires people to come to grips with the finality of death when a friend, family member, or leader passes on. Funerals provide people with this opportunity, allowing them to say goodbye and freeing them to move on with their lives.

However, the people of Israel didn't have this opportunity when Moses died. Not only had they lost their beloved leader, but since they didn't know where his dead body was located, they'd also lost the opportunity to say goodbye to him. It must have felt like a double loss. Deuteronomy 34:8 relates their sorrow, saying, "And the children of Israel wept for Moses in the plains of Moab thirty days: so the days of weeping and mourning for Moses were ended."

THE GREATEST PROPHET
OF THE OLD TESTAMENT

Everyone knew Moses was a special man of God unlike any other. He was so special, in fact, that Deuteronomy 34:10 tells us, "...There arose not a prophet since in Israel like unto Moses, whom the Lord knew face to face."

Moses' life was uncommonly unique in the history of mankind. Born a Hebrew, he was adopted as an infant by Pharaoh's daughter and then raised as an Egyptian. As an adult, Moses converted to the Hebrew faith and later delivered the children of Israel from Egyptian slavery. Moses was bold, courageous, and mightily anointed by God. Defying the power of Egypt with only a rod in his hand, he brought down supernatural plagues upon that oppressive nation when the pharaoh of Egypt refused to let God's people go free.

Moses had the divine authority to command the waters of the Nile to turn into blood and the sand into lice. He brought swarming hordes of locusts to eat the crops of Egypt, and he called down fire and hail from the heavens. With the Egyptian armies at his back, Moses commanded the Red Sea to part, and God separated the sea into towering walls of churning water. Moses was chosen to receive God's laws and confer them to His people. And in the entire history of humanity, he was the only man ever to catch a glimpse of the actual body of God (*see* Exodus 33:23).

Moses was in a category of all his own as a God-called man. He was one of a kind, truly unique and special in both his anointing and the types of miracles God performed through him. Thus, it was a terrible tragedy for Israel when he died.

Furthermore, Moses had been Israel's only contact with God for more than 40 years. If they needed to say something to God, they sent Moses to speak to Him on their behalf. And when God wanted to speak to His people, He spoke to Moses, and Moses related God's message to the children of Israel.

Moses represented the presence and the voice of God to the nation of Israel. He was the prophet of God, the intercessor for the people, and the mediator between God and man. Therefore, when Moses died, the Israelites grieved because they had lost not only a dear friend and leader, but also their representation before God.

Feeling hopeless and desperate, the people of Israel wondered, *What will we do without Moses? How will we hear from God? Who will intercede with God on our behalf? Where will we find food and water? And who will deliver us from our next enemy?*

Because Moses had been God's instrument, a huge spiritual vacuum had been created in the wake of the leader's death. The Israelites were naturally scared and uncertain about their future. But in the midst of this environment of fear and doubt, God was already preparing to raise up a new leader to lead His children into the Promised Land.

Joshua 1:1 continues, "Now after the death of Moses the servant of the Lord it came to pass, that the Lord spake unto Joshua...."

Joshua was God's choice to succeed Moses as the leader of Israel.

Your Day Finally Arrives!

Let me ask you the same question I asked you in the introduction of Chapter One: Have you ever earnestly longed for something and prayed so fervently for it that every cell and fiber of your being waited in anticipation to receive the answer to your prayer? And then suddenly *it happens*! Things begin moving so quickly that you feel like your head is swimming!

All your years of waiting and all the grueling hours you spent training are suddenly called upon, and your faith must rise to the occasion to accept a new position in the Kingdom of God. There's no time to pray or think about whether or not you should accept this new assignment. You've been praying about it and waiting for it for years! This is your time. This is your hour. *Your day has finally arrived!*

That kind of excitement and anxiety must have been exactly what Joshua felt when he realized that his hour to lead Israel had finally come. For decades, Joshua had served Moses and had been groomed by God to accept Moses' position. And then suddenly, *it happened*! In a flash, Moses was gone, and Joshua was promoted to the highest position of leadership in God's plan.

In an instant, the spotlight that had been focused on Moses for an entire generation abruptly shifted to Joshua. Joshua now found himself standing in front of several million Israelites, all of whom were probably wondering, *Will he ever be the kind of leader Moses was?*

How would you have felt that day if you had been Joshua? Imagine the pressure he must have felt as he stepped before that immense crowd of grieving Israelites. I can almost hear Joshua's heart pounding as he stood there looking into the eyes of the multitudes who stared back at him intently — each of them thinking, *Can he do it? Can he lead us? Will he be like Moses?*

Moses would be a hard act to follow!

Think about it! What if Moses had been your pastor? It would be very difficult to settle for someone else, wouldn't it? If your pastor was accompanied by a pillar of fire and billows of smoke every time he came to church, it would be a great letdown to lose him!

Naturally speaking, who would want to try to fill the shoes of Moses? Moses had been Israel's pastor, prophet, leader, and, to many, a beloved friend for 40 years. Besides that, he was known to have had God's ear and to have moved in His power. Whether or not the Israelites liked Moses, they couldn't dispute his God-given position and authority.

To complicate matters even more, people who are faced with the death of a friend or loved one often tend to quickly forget that individual's flaws and weaknesses and choose instead to dwell his or her strengths. This was no doubt the case with the Israelites in the wake of Moses' death. Within days of their leader's passing, the children of Israel probably began to exaggerate Moses' good qualities and raise him up to a superhuman level in their minds. They probably said things like, "There will never be another Moses. I don't know how we can go on without him. No one will ever walk in the anointing Moses walked in or do the miracles he did."

If there ever was a time for feeling inadequate and incapable, it was when Joshua faced the Hebrew nation for the first time as their new leader. Even Joshua must have wondered, *Am I fit for the task? Can I do this?* Mixed emotions probably raged through his natural mind, shouting, *Go for it!* one moment and, *You're crazy!* the next. If he was a normal human being like you and me,

Joshua's spirit was erupting with joy at the chance to be God's leader. But his flesh probably wanted to slow down and think about the situation for a few more days!

This was Joshua's point of no return. He couldn't turn back, slow down, or pass the buck to someone else. He had been training and preparing for this moment for years, and now that moment had suddenly burst upon him. This was it! *His day had finally arrived!*

> This was Joshua's point of no return. He had been training and preparing for this moment for years, and now that moment had suddenly burst upon him.

When Joshua stood and looked out onto the masses of people in his new congregation, reality hit him hard and fast. He was being required to move up his degree of commitment to a higher, more intense level.

Life as he had known it was gone forever.

ARE YOU READY FOR *YOUR* NEW ASSIGNMENT IN LIFE?

When God opens huge doors of opportunity for you, you may ask, *Am I ready for this? Can I handle this kind of responsibility? Am I spiritually mature enough to deal with all that comes with this kind of position?*

Those are good questions to ask, but consider this: If God Himself has truly opened a door of opportunity for you, He has obviously counted you faithful enough at this point in your life to handle a new assignment. Otherwise, the door wouldn't be open to you. So if you don't think you're mature enough to handle what God has asked you to do, don't worry! You can rest assured that He will help you mature and grow as you stay on the path He's ordained for you. (I recommend that you read my book, *If You Were God, Would You Choose You?*)

If you wait until you think you're completely prepared to begin your next assignment, you'll probably never do anything significant for the Kingdom of God because you'll never really feel like you're "ready." Most likely, you won't feel good enough, prepared enough, or mature enough to handle that new assignment.

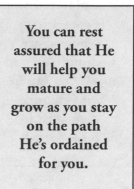

You can rest assured that He will help you mature and grow as you stay on the path He's ordained for you.

If a door opens and you hear God beckoning you to walk through, just trust His judgment over your own concerning your "readiness." You're not a good judge of your ability to be used by Him anyway! Remember, even the apostle Paul said, "...Yea, I judge not mine own self" (1 Corinthians 4:3). Of course, you should judge yourself in matters of discipline, financial responsibility, how you treat others, and so on. But you should never judge whether you're ready for a new task in the Kingdom of God — especially if it's a big one!

When you look at the immensity of the assignment God is asking you to do, you may feel very small and ill-equipped for the task. But that isn't entirely bad! As long as your feelings of inadequacy don't prevent you from accepting God's new assignment, those same insecure feelings may ultimately be very beneficial to you. It's actually good to realize your dependence upon God as you initiate a major new step in your life. It's only when you become cocky and arrogant — so reliant upon yourself that you forget your need for God's strength — that you can fail.

However, it's important not to confuse genuine humility with *false* humility. A person with false humility continually talks about his unworthiness to take on a task God has given him. On the other hand, true humility is demonstrated when a person recognizes his inadequacy to do the job but accepts God's plan and trusts that he can get it done with the Lord's help.

> *Real humility is recognizing who you are without God and what you can be if you put your trust in Jesus Christ.*

Real humility is recognizing who you are without God and what you can be if you put your trust in Jesus Christ.

The truth is, naturally speaking, you aren't worthy of your new assignment. Big deal! According to the natural, you weren't worthy to receive your salvation either. Nor were you worthy to receive the infilling of the Holy Spirit, healing, or answers to your prayers. In fact, Romans 3:20 states that according to your own deeds and actions, you're not worthy of anything except eternal judgment!

However, your unworthiness didn't change the fact that God chose you, saved you, healed you, and answered your prayers time and time again. You didn't deserve any of this, yet because His work in your life is a work of grace, you received all of it anyway. You're a recipient of God's wonderworking grace!

Because of God's grace, you can realistically look at the inadequacies you feel and confidently proclaim, "I can do all things through Christ which strengtheneth me" (Philippians 4:13). In fact, this verse could be translated, *"I can do all things through Christ, who infuses me with a brand-new, continuous stream of fresh power each new day."*

This daily inflow of fresh power comes from having a vibrant, working relationship with the Lord Jesus Christ. Your dependence on Him in that relationship is the key to receiving the daily infusion of divine strength and wisdom that will enable you to accept and victoriously fulfill God's next assignment for your life.

You may not feel ready for your next new assignment from God, but that's all right. When *God* thinks you're ready, He provides the grace and power to *make* you ready. He will mature and equip you for the task. God just wants to hear your heart say *yes* to the next exciting phase of life He is placing before you.

> **When God thinks you're ready, He provides the grace and power to *make* you ready.**

The Apostle Paul Faced the Point of No Return

The apostle Paul faced the point of no return on at least two separate occasions. The first was the moment Jesus appeared to him on the road to Damascus, and the second occurred on his first journey to Corinth. That second point of no return was a very difficult and painful place for Paul, but on the other side of that landmark moment, Paul was set on course for a tremendous, supernatural ministry.

In First Corinthians 2:1-3, Paul described his state of mind as he faced that second point of no return. He wrote, "And I, brethren, when I came to you, came not with excellency of speech or of wisdom, declaring unto you the testimony of God. For I determined not to know any thing among you, save Jesus Christ, and him crucified. And I was with you in weakness, and in fear, and in much trembling."

In these three verses, Paul revealed his spiritual condition when he first arrived in Corinth — a journey that had been preceded by a very painful period of ministry. Consider what Paul had just gone through:

- He had been confronted with angry unbelievers in Pisidian Antioch and then forcibly expelled from their city (*see* Acts 13:50).

- He had to flee from Iconium to escape being stoned by an angry mob (*see* Acts 14:6).

- That angry mob followed him to Lystra, where he was nearly stoned to death, surviving the ordeal only because faithful Christians encircled his lifeless body and asked God to raise him from the dead (*see* Acts 14:20).

- He had been flogged, imprisoned, and rioted against in Philippi (*see* Acts 16:22,23).

- He had been chased out of Thessalonica by violent criminals (*see* Acts 17:5).

- He had almost been assaulted by angry Jews in Berea (*see* Acts 17:13).

- He had faced mocking philosophers in Athens (*see* Acts 17:32).

It was after this succession of harrowing experiences that the apostle Paul headed to Corinth — a city infamous for its sexual perversion and demonic activity. As he walked over the hills toward the city of Corinth, Paul was thinking about the direction of his ministry. Naturally speaking, things weren't going very well! He had been stoned, beaten, imprisoned, and thrown out of several cities. Everywhere Paul went, he had infuriated Jews and pagans alike, and despite his best efforts, the response to his message had been weak at best.

With all of this in mind, notice how Paul begins verse 3: "And I was with you...." The word "with" is taken from the Greek word *pros,* which nearly always describes a face-to-face situation. Knowing this, the verse could be translated, *"And when I was face to face with you...."*

Because Paul used this word *pros* ("face to face"), we know that he was reflecting on the time when he and the Corinthians first laid eyes on each other. At that time, they were pagans, immersed in sexual debauchery and depravity. Paul vividly recalled that moment when he stood before these pagans because that was his point of no return. Let me explain.

Up to this point in his ministry, Paul had relied on his own natural abilities and understanding as he endeavored to preach the Gospel. He was a highly educated, intelligent man with an innate gift for debating. So when he traveled to new cities, Paul primarily attempted to convince his audience of the truth of the Gospel through reasoned, well-crafted arguments. But instead of bringing great multitudes of people to Christ, this strategy merely reaped intense opposition. When his powerful mind took on pagan and Jewish audiences — passionately arguing and reasoning with them — Paul made them so angry that they actually wanted to kill him!

On that journey to Corinth, Paul no doubt reflected on his past difficulties and probably wondered what kind of trouble he would drum up next. One thing had become crystal clear: Ministering from his own natural ability was not producing a lot of good fruit! Maybe it was time to let the Holy Spirit take over completely.

It was at this point in Paul's ministry that he came to a place of absolute surrender to the power of the Holy Spirit. This decision was his point of no return. There would be no turning back from this new commitment. Paul later described this moment of rock-solid resolution to the Corinthian believers, saying, "And I, brethren, when I came to you, came not with excellency of speech or of wisdom, declaring unto you the testimony of God. For I determined not to know anything among you, save Jesus Christ, and him crucified" (1 Corinthians 2:1,2).

Rather than relying on his own abilities and intellect, Paul decided to put his trust solely in the Holy Spirit. From that moment onward, he stopped trying to debate, reason, and argue with his audience, but chose instead to simply preach *Jesus Christ and Him crucified.* No more overly complex preaching was going to come from this man of God — only the Gospel in its purest and simplest form.

Now, this might sound like a simple decision, and for a simple person, it may have indeed been an easy choice. But Paul was not a simple person! He was a complicated intellectual with great natural ability. Choosing to deny his own persuasive abilities and keep his mind quiet in order to preach a simple, straightforward message — without arguing or debating — was a monumental step for Paul. Nevertheless, that was the commitment he had made out on those hills as he walked toward Corinth.

> **The hard reality of these decisions always hits us when we leave our private place of prayer to face life head-on.**

Making life-changing decisions is sometimes easier to do when we are alone, whether walking through the hills or at home in our prayer closets. *But the hard reality of these decisions always hits us when we leave our private place of prayer to face life head-on.* That's when we must follow through on our resolutions — and when we find out whether or not we were really serious about them! This is true for any area of our lives, no matter how important or insignificant the decision might seem.

For instance, let's say you're lying in bed one night and you say to yourself, *Tomorrow I'm going to start a new diet.* Then tomorrow comes, and your friends invite you over for a big, juicy hamburger with lots of delicious, greasy french fries. That's the moment you face your point of no return head-on! You'll find out then whether you were really serious about your commitment to change or your decision was merely a wishy-washy fantasy.

Paul made his decision alone in the hills on his journey to Corinth. But when he first arrived in that city and began to preach in public — gazing upon a crowd of staring faces — he suddenly became aware of the seriousness of his choice.

In the past, he could have easily resorted to his natural powers of persuasion, rhetorical abilities, and intellectual prowess — but no longer. He had made a commitment to the Lord, and he was serious about carrying it out. Paul couldn't speak to them with "...excellency of speech or of wisdom, declaring unto...[them] the testimony of God..." (1 Corinthians 2:1). Nor could he determine "...to know any thing among...[them], save Jesus Christ and him crucified" (1 Corinthians 2:2).

Thus, when Paul found himself face to face with the Corinthians, he stood there "...in weakness, and in fear, and in much trembling" (1 Corinthians 2:3). This is what Paul felt at that critical moment. As he looked into the faces of those Corinthian pagans, he knew that if God didn't do something wonderful soon, he was in big trouble! Paul felt a new helplessness and utter dependence on the power of the Holy Spirit. Most likely, he was tempted to lapse back into his previous mode of ministry, but that was no longer an option. *Paul had crossed the point of no return.*

WEAKNESS, FEAR, AND MUCH TREMBLING

Notice that Paul said, "And I was with you *in weakness, and in fear, and in much trembling*" (1 Corinthians 2:3). Today this kind of statement would be seen as a lack of faith in many Christian circles. But in fact, this attitude of "weakness," "fear," and "much trembling" was the very perspective that launched Paul into a powerful faith ministry!

"Weakness," "fear," and "much trembling" may not sound like the characteristics of a man of faith and power, but they are nonetheless. Allow me to explain.

I know great men and women of God from all across the world. They have mountain-moving faith, and they regularly witness God perform incredible, breathtaking signs and wonders. Yet naturally speaking, they still have to deal with "weakness," "fear," and "much trembling" every time they stand up to minister. This fact may surprise some people because these same ministers appear to be so bold and courageous when they are operating under the anointing of the Holy Spirit. But even as they operate in miraculous realms of faith that literally amaze their audience, God-called ministers often struggle personally with feelings of uncertainty.

Let me give you a hypothetical example of what I mean. A preacher steps onto the stage to minister to thousands of sick people. He is fully aware that many of them have driven or flown hundreds or even thousands of miles to come to his healing service. They are all expecting to receive their healing that very night, and that minister is their point of contact to receive a miracle from God. This awareness creates an overwhelming sense of responsibility in the soul of that preacher — very much like the feeling of "weakness," "fear," and "much trembling" Paul described.

When that minister looks out into the crowd and sees the great needs and the expectations of the masses, he knows that some will die if they aren't healed that night. He knows that only God can meet every need, heal every sick body, and mend every heart, and he is fully aware that if the Holy Spirit doesn't move in that meeting in a powerful way, many people will return home sad, disappointed, and still sick. The knowledge that only God can do these miracles creates an utter dependence on the Holy Spirit in the heart of that minister.

When God tells you to do something, it will usually require a big leap of faith.

Rarely do you have the comfort of doing something for God that seems small in your own eyes. Most often when He speaks a word to your heart, you will think He is asking you to take the biggest leap of faith you've ever taken in your life, even if it looks small to someone else.

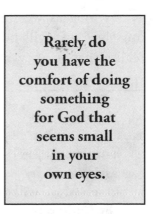

Rarely do you have the comfort of doing something for God that seems small in your own eyes.

That's how Denise and I felt when we first began to travel in the mid-'80s in order to teach the Word of God across the United States. We were so new and unknown that we had only five meetings booked over a period of two months. Actually, at the time, we were amazed we even had five! Everybody at home told us that five meetings would never cover two months of travel expenses and that we would go broke on the road. But we knew that the Lord had spoken to us and that the mantle was on us to go.

So Denise and I set out — and we had five glorious meetings! It was a giant step of faith for us, but we didn't have a choice because we had passed the point of no return. As it turned out, those five meetings laid a foundation for our ministry that eventually brought us more than 900 invitations a year. But when we first stepped out to obey God, I definitely felt weakness, fear, and much trembling!

When your next new assignment begins — whether it is your next job, your next pastorate, your next school year, or your next project — you might also feel a little "weakness," "fear," and "much trembling." If this is the case, you've probably realized that you've stepped into something much bigger than you could have imagined and that the success of the entire endeavor rests on *your* shoulders. Knowing that you absolutely cannot make a mistake will cause you to feel a deep need for God to step in and help you get the job done!

As long as we think we can handle a divine assignment by ourselves, we will be limited to our own ability. But when we realize that our new assignment in life is just too big to handle on our own, we have no choice but to move beyond ourselves into the dimension of God Himself.

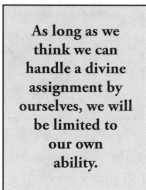

As long as we think we can handle a divine assignment by ourselves, we will be limited to our own ability.

We know from the book of Acts and from Church history that Paul's ministry in Corinth was very successful. Literally thousands of people were saved and filled with the Holy Spirit. And although some believers in Corinth struggled to completely separate themselves from the sinful lifestyles of their past, the Corinthian congregation was renowned for the mighty gifts and moves of the Spirit that constantly operated in their midst.

Let's consider the example of Joshua for a moment. Like Paul when he walked into Corinth, Joshua faced the nation of Israel for the first time with feelings of weakness, fear, and much trembling. Just the knowledge that he was following in the footsteps of Moses should have been enough to make Joshua want to turn and run for the hills! But like Paul, Joshua had made a commitment to the Lord, and it was time to move ahead. This characteristic of pushing past natural feelings of inadequacy to move forward in one's divine assignment is the mark of a great man or woman of God and a great leader.

We Are All Called To Lead

As you've been reading this teaching, you may have thought, *I'm not called to be a minister or the president of a large company or anything like that. What does all this leadership stuff have to do with me?*

If that's what you're thinking, I challenge you to closely examine your life. When you do, I guarantee that you'll find areas in your life in which you've been called to be a leader. For example:

- Husbands are called to lead their marriages as the head of their households (*see* Ephesians 5:23).

- Wives are called to help their husbands train, teach, and lead their children.

- Older children are called to help guide younger children.

- Employers are called to lead their employees, who in turn often lead other employees.

- And most importantly, God has called every Christian, regardless of his or her position in life, to make disciples of other believers (*see* Matthew 28:19).

Therefore, when I discuss "leadership" in this book, I'm not just referring to being in full-time ministry or running a business. The common sense and wisdom found in this teaching can be applied to any walk of life you may find yourself in.

We all find ourselves in the chain of authority, and submission is the name of the game! No matter whom we may be leading, we all have people who are in authority over us as well. And whether we're called to be a leader or a follower in any given realm of life, we're first and foremost servants of Christ Jesus. *He is our Ultimate Authority!*

> **Whether we're called to be a leader or a follower in any given realm of life, we're first and foremost servants of Christ Jesus.**

FOLLOWING IN THE FOOTSTEPS OF ANOTHER LEADER

Before closing this chapter, I want to address another issue you may face when God promotes you into a new position of leadership — *the challenge of following in the steps of another leader.*

If your predecessor was a poor leader — perhaps proving to be irresponsible, immoral, unethical, or lacking in honesty and integrity — you will have the challenge of winning your people's trust and respect. This process takes time, patience, and perseverance, but eventually you can win their hearts through your own good example.

On the other hand, if your predecessor was a good leader with a long tenure, the experience of trying to fill his or her shoes can be just as difficult and painful — *if not more so.* People who were happy and prosperous under their previous leader may be resistant to change and thus unwilling to adjust to your personality and style of doing things.

But we must remember that *any of us* who truly seek to move higher in our walk with God could face this kind of situation at some point in our lives and that we therefore need to mentally prepare ourselves. This is true whether we're anticipating a promotion in business, replacing a retired or deceased pastor in ministry, or involved in any other life situation that requires a transfer of leadership.

For instance, when a church has had one pastor for many years and then that pastor suddenly retires or dies, it's very common for the next pastor to have a very short term there. The new pastor may be excellent, perhaps even better equipped than his predecessor. But because his way of doing things isn't identical to that of the previous pastor, the congregation may not receive him well. They're accustomed to another leadership style. Consequently, it could be hard for the new pastor to quickly make the necessary adjustments needed to succeed in his new role.

Change almost always seems threatening to people, and new leadership represents change.

When a new pastor is called to a church, the congregation may make every effort to be open-minded, accepting, and gracious. But every time that new leader steps into the pulpit to preach for the first month or so, most church members, whether consciously or unconsciously, will inevitably compare their new pastor to their old one. Thus, it's common for a church to go through two or three new pastors before they settle down with a pastor who sticks it out and builds his own, unique ministry with them.

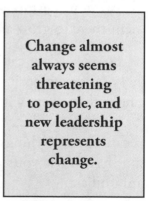

Change almost always seems threatening to people, and new leadership represents change.

The same principle is true in the realms of business and politics as well. New leaders — whether new presidents, new congressmen, new employers, and so on — are always compared to their predecessors. It's the nature of human beings to watch, compare, talk about, and test their new leadership. This is one reason why following in the steps of a strong leader can be a challenging and often frustrating experience. Think about how many times you've heard someone say, "Our other boss didn't do it that way! I don't know why we have to change. We've always done it this way, and it's always worked."

Nevertheless, God will use these times of change and transition to change people's hearts.

For instance, if a congregation is struggling with a new pastor's way of doing things, they may need to get honest before God and acknowledge that they're stuck in a rut and need to be more flexible and open to change. At the same time, the new pastor's leadership skills will also be revealed as he navigates this time of transition.

This time of trial and testing ultimately makes it clear whether or not the new pastor has the anointing and guts to lead that local church into the future. If he does, it will quickly become apparent which church members attended the church because they liked the previous pastor and which ones are there because God called them there to grow and serve, no matter who the leader may be.

So if God is calling you to a new assignment in life that includes a new position of leadership, be realistic about the challenges that come with your new task. You will be compared to the previous leader; your methods and style might be questioned because you do things differently; and you may be misunderstood simply because your personality and leadership style is new and unfamiliar.

But remember — that's just human nature! If you have the courage to face your new assignment head-on and keep moving forward, you'll prove your dedication and seriousness to those under your leadership. You'll demonstrate through your actions that you're really called by God and that you truly care about them. Most importantly, as you persevere in faith, God will give you supernatural favor with those around you. Eventually they'll learn to trust and follow you just as ardently as they did their last leader.

> **As you persevere in faith, God will give you supernatural favor with those around you.**

Think About It

It's important to evaluate and assess before you make a decision. However, evaluation is only helpful when the witness of God's Spirit and the confirmation of His Word are what you use to measure and determine what to do. Your abilities and personal resources will never be enough. Only when the will of God is factored into the equation will you come to the right conclusion.

Within God's specific word to your heart regarding His plan for you, you will find the answer or the approach you need to address the challenges or concerns that stand between you and your next step. What has God called you to do? Along with that command, what promises has He given you? Dedicate yourself to praying about what God has said to you. As you do, you will gain insight into His divine strategy with specific steps you need to take to get from "here" to "there."

❧

God-breathed confidence will hold you steady even when you "feel" inadequate. As you prepare to move forward from one season into the next, you need to remember what God spoke to your heart when you were praying so that confusion can't cloud your thoughts with emotions during times of planning and preparing to step out.

What specific scriptures has God given you that help define this particular "point of no return" in your life?

CHAPTER THREE

PASSING THE LEADERSHIP TEST

What do you think causes God to promote some people into positions of leadership and not others?

To answer that question, consider *these* questions:

- If you were looking for leaders, what would you look for?

- What would be the main qualities that would catch your attention?

- If you were God, would you choose someone like you?

To answer these questions, you must look further at Joshua 1:1. It reads, "Now after the death of Moses the servant of the Lord it came to pass, that the Lord spake unto Joshua, the son of Nun, Moses' minister...." I want you to particularly notice the last part of the verse, which says, "...The Lord spake unto Joshua, the son of Nun, *Moses' minister*...."

Here we find a tremendous key that reveals why God chose Joshua: *because Joshua was Moses' minister.* Other translators have rendered the word "minister" as *associate, assistant, disciple,* or *servant.* This is very important because it shows that one of the marks of a great leader is his willingness to obediently and faithfully follow those who are in authority over him.

Moreover, by referring to Joshua as "Moses' minister," this verse reveals that Joshua wasn't an unknown, mysterious figure when God chose him to replace Moses. Joshua had been around for a long time, and he had a proven track record. For decades, Joshua had faithfully served as Moses' associate, assistant, disciple, and servant.

During Joshua's time as an associate, he'd probably done many menial and unnoticed tasks, and occasionally he may have even felt used by Moses. Moses was a busy man with many responsibilities. Therefore, Joshua — like most associates or assistants of strong leaders — probably did a lot of dirty work and received very little glory. But that wasn't necessarily a bad thing. Periods of serving are testing grounds that prove whether or not an associate has the strength of character to be a leader himself.

> **Periods of serving are testing grounds that prove whether or not an associate has the strength of character to be a leader himself.**

If a person can't follow, he isn't ready to lead!

Furthermore, when you serve in a subordinate position, you'll usually have to wrestle with fleshly feelings of being neglected or unappreciated by others. Yet God will use this internal wrestling match to expose the right or wrong motives in your heart. He'll find out why you are *really* serving the Lord.

- Do you serve Him to obtain glory in the eyes of others?

- Or do you serve Him with pure motives in your current capacity, simply because that's what He has asked you to do?

One of the most important things for any associate or employee to discover is the condition of his or her own heart.

Many times the best way to do this is by serving in a position that doesn't gain any recognition.

Those who work under strong leaders can find it very difficult at times. However, the Holy Spirit will help them through their challenges by encouraging and teaching them how to develop humble hearts and minds.

Leaders who have learned how to maintain an attitude of humility have made many mistakes in the past — and they will no doubt continue to make many more in the future. Yet because these leaders' hearts are right toward God and men, God will guide them through every calamity or obstacle, instructing them in their error and giving them the grace and favor to continue and succeed.

A strong example of this principle is found in the life of King David. David made many mistakes throughout his reign as king, some of which were major errors. But he maintained an attitude of humility and submission toward God — and that profound humility gave David a stature of greatness that far exceeded all the other kings of Israel.

In First Peter 5:5, the apostle Peter wrote about the importance of humility and submission in the Church, exhorting, "Likewise, ye younger, submit yourselves unto the elder. Yea, all of you be subject one to another, and be clothed with humility: for God resisteth the proud, and giveth grace to the humble."

Submitting to authority is always a big test, and it's an especially vital one for leaders. A person serving under a leader may be tempted to think from time to time that he's been asked to do something that is beneath him. Perhaps he thinks the task at hand is too basic and menial for someone as greatly anointed, talented, or intelligent as he is. If so, that person needs to remind himself that those thoughts are just the complaints of his flesh, and then he should tell his flesh to shut up!

Some scholars suggest that when Peter admonished us to "be clothed with humility," he was remembering the Last Supper when Jesus Himself took off His own outer garment and stooped down to wash the feet of His disciples. Think about it — the Lord of Glory was willing to wash the dirty feet of His disciples right before He died for them!

Since Jesus was willing to do that, we should always make it our aim to "be clothed with humility." This means we are to faithfully serve those whom God has called us to serve, even when we think the task at hand is menial or boring.

A FAITHFUL SERVANT

Let me explain what the word "faithfully" means in this context of *faithfulness* in our relationships and in the tasks assigned to us. Faithfulness means being thorough, consistent, loyal, and true to one's word. *It's the consistent outward manifestation of a humble heart.*

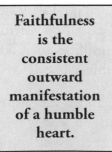

Faithfulness is the consistent outward manifestation of a humble heart.

Joshua is a prime Old Testament example of an individual who consistently proved himself faithful. Throughout all the adversity and challenges he faced together with Moses, Joshua stayed in his place at his leader's side, assisting and serving Moses and the people of Israel for many years.

Furthermore, in Second Timothy 2:2, we see that Paul instructed Timothy to choose leaders who were "...faithful men, who shall be able to teach others also." It's important to note that Paul didn't tell Timothy to choose *talented* or *capable* men.

Rather, he said to choose *faithful* men for notable positions of leadership in the Church.

In order for a leader to determine whether or not a person is faithful, that person must be tested. Faithfulness is about passing the tests of time by remaining committed to one's assignment, being loyal in one's relationships, and submitting to authority. There must be a multitude of tests and challenges over a prolonged period of time to truly establish whether or not a person is faithful.

This is precisely why Paul told Timothy, "Lay hands suddenly on no man..." (1 Timothy 5:22). As the old saying goes, all that glitters is not gold! Likewise, not everyone who looks good to the eye and sounds impressive is necessarily the one you want to serve alongside you in your ministry or place of business. Remember, the serpent was more cunning than any beast of the field (*see* Genesis 3:1) — and Satan used it to destroy the paradise of God.

The Bible tells us that Moses' trust for Joshua grew throughout the years of their association. The last chapter of Deuteronomy relates, "And Joshua the son of Nun was full of the spirit of wisdom; for Moses had laid his hands upon him..." (Deuteronomy 34:9). Through the laying on of hands, Moses not only confirmed God's call upon Joshua, but also acknowledged Joshua's faithfulness.

When Joshua first stood before the nation of Israel as their new leader who would lead them into the Promised Land, he had already acquired all these marks of leadership. He had proven himself faithful; he had established an attitude of humility; and he had shown his willingness to stick it out with the Israelites despite their often stubborn and rebellious attitude.

Joshua had learned much from his mentor, Moses — both what to do and what not to do. Whether or not Joshua agreed with every one of Moses' decisions, he had served Moses as an able minister without complaint and thus proved himself worthy of taking on new and greater responsibilities.

FLAWS, IMPERFECTIONS, AND UNREALISTIC EXPECTATIONS

Serving under a mighty man of God is a "two-edged sword." On one hand, you constantly have before you a vivid example of someone who has been chosen by God to lead His people. As such, you're able to see firsthand an incredible vision brought forth and take form. You'll probably also witness tremendous miracles and hear revelation from God's Word expounded in an awesome, powerful, life-transforming way.

On the other hand, you'll also witness a clear example of an imperfect human being. As you draw close to that person, you'll begin to see his character, his personality, the way he handles himself in all kinds of situations, and how he reacts to different people. And when everything is revealed, you may not like what you see!

At that point, you'll undoubtedly have to look inward and assess your motivations for serving. You'll have to ask yourself, *Am I serving this leader to share his glory and reputation, gain approval, and advance my own ministry — or am I serving him as unto the Lord (see* Colossians 3:23)?

Let's go back to the example of Joshua and Moses. We tend to focus on all of Moses' good points, and there's nothing wrong with that. But let's think about it for a moment. What would it really have been like to work under Moses?

Moses was the man who, with God's help, had called down plagues on the land of Egypt, parted the Red Sea, and destroyed Pharaoh and his armies. Moses had stood in the presence of God on Mt. Sinai, and he had even seen the hind parts of God while God covered him with His own hand. What a story! No one else could boast of such an impressive, awe-inspiring resume!

However, Moses had very pronounced character flaws as well. His personality was so strong that it caused him to seek complete control over his ministry and to try to do everything himself. In fact, the situation got so bad at one point that Moses' father-in-law, Jethro, rebuked him and told him to start delegating authority to other people before it killed him (*see* Exodus 18:13-27).

Scripture also reveals that Moses could be very impatient. When God specifically instructed him to strike a rock one time and the water didn't come out as quickly as Moses wished, Moses threw a temper tantrum and struck the rock in anger a second time — defying the order of God. It was because of this act of anger that he was barred from entering the Promised Land (*see* Numbers 20:7-12).

All of this goes to show that although Moses was a mighty prophet of God, he was also a real human being with real imperfections!

Why do I share this? Because believers often have unrealistic expectations of anointed leadership. Many times Christians think that because their leaders are equipped to stand in their call, they are immune from human responses to the challenges of daily life. People assume that being anointed somehow translates into being exempt from carnality and fleshly reactions.

We need to adjust our unrealistic expectations! *People are people.* Although we must respect the call of God on our spiritual leaders and recognize that God promoted them into the position they hold, we must also allow them to function as normal human beings. It's a false illusion to believe that they do nothing but pray and prophesy and sound spiritual all day long. Of course they can never live up to that kind of expectation!

The apostle Paul was very straightforward about his own humanity, and he wrote about the struggles he faced in his personal life on several occasions. In Second Corinthians 4:7, he said, "...We have this treasure in earthen vessels, that the excellency of the power may be of God, and not of us." This verse reveals that Paul was keenly aware of his own human weaknesses, as well as the infinite value of the gifts God had placed in him despite his imperfections.

Notice that Paul said, "...We have this *treasure in earthen vessels....*" This word "treasure" comes from the Greek word *theasauros*, which describes *an inexhaustible supply of riches*. By using this word, Paul was proclaiming — almost in amazement — that he had within himself an inexhaustible spiritual treasure! He then went on to say that this inexhaustible spiritual treasure resides in "earthen vessels."

The word "earthen" comes from the word *ostrikinos*, which describes *a material so fragile that it will break and fall to pieces in one's hands if it's handled too roughly*. Paul was telling us that this "inexhaustible spiritual treasure" lives inside a fragile, breakable vessel. What an astonishing fact it is that God would place such riches inside of something as temporal and fragile as us!

Paul knew that God's gifts resided in his life. But he was just as aware that his human body was nothing more than an "earthen vessel." That fact didn't minimize the treasure within him; rather, it just put things in their proper perspective.

Although our leaders are richly anointed and gifted by God, they still live in earthen vessels that are far from perfect. Thus, we shouldn't be surprised when imperfect vessels occasionally behave imperfectly.

The Bible abounds with examples of great spiritual leaders who made big mistakes as they tried to walk in faith and follow God. We see human imperfections in Abraham, who often struggled in his walk of faith; we find imperfections in David, who committed both adultery and murder; and we can read about the flaws of the powerful prophet Elijah, who destroyed the prophets of Baal one day and then ran from Queen Jezebel in total panic the next.

Our behavior may not always be the way we want it to be, but we have to keep in mind that we're *human.* And if we spent time around the spiritual leaders we admire and respect, we'd see that they have flaws and weaknesses as well. Until we all see Jesus Christ face to face and are completely and permanently changed into His image, we'll still have room for improvement in our faith, our character, and our lives.

AN IMPORTANT LEADERSHIP TEST

If you ever serve under a spiritual leader, you will undergo a big test to see how you respond to that leader's humanity. Ultimately, if you judge him for being imperfect, you're not mature enough to move into leadership yourself. You're only setting yourself up for a terrible fall.

> Until we all see Jesus Christ face to face and are completely and permanently changed into His image, we'll still have room for improvement in our faith, our character, and our lives.

However, if you do pass this strategic leadership test, you'll have overcome one of the most difficult hurdles you'll probably ever encounter. And on the other side of the test, you'll be on your way to becoming someone God can use powerfully in this world.

When you see your leader move in the power of God, you may tend to forget that he's just a human being. You might put him on a pedestal in your mind, set apart from average people in some exalted category. But that unrealistic expectation will wear off very quickly as you work closely with him.

Up close, the blemishes that aren't readily apparent in your leader will begin to become evident, and the devil will try to use those character flaws to discourage, distract, and deter you from submitting to the man of God you've been called to serve. If you have unrealistic expectations of the person God has placed over you, his faults and weaknesses can come as a shock to your system! In the end, you'll choose to either be offended or to forgive him, pray for him, and serve him in an even more excellent manner.

It's clear to me that Joshua must have passed this strategic leadership test. He not only worked with Moses, but he also walked with him, served him, and stayed with him through all the ups and downs of the time they spent together.

The same could *not* be said about me. Personally, I had a tremendous struggle with this test. When I was a very young man, I served on the staff of a large Southern Baptist church. In my estimation, the pastor was one of the best Bible teachers in the United States at the time. I respected and admired this man immensely because he read Greek, knew Hebrew, and taught the Word of God verse by verse like a Bible scholar — and he also believed in the infilling of the Holy Spirit!

Having been reared in the sound doctrines of the Southern Baptist denomination and then baptized in the Holy Spirit as a teenager, I had hungered to follow a man of God who brought sound doctrine and supernatural power together in ministry. In my thinking, this was the finest combination I could desire!

When I first began attending the large church this man pastored, I would sit on the front row every week, mesmerized by his teaching from the Scriptures. *Surely*, I thought, *This man's style of teaching must be similar to the teaching of the apostle Paul.* With all my being, I yearned to know this pastor inside and out, to work with him, to assist him, and to serve him. I was willing to do any menial labor or task in order to be close to that kind of wisdom and anointing.

Finally, the day came when God opened the door for me to join the staff of this pastor's church. One of my new responsibilities was to strengthen a division of the Sunday school that had been weak; the other part of my job was to be an assistant to the pastor and do whatever he needed me to do. I was absolutely thrilled!

It wasn't long before my Sunday school division began to grow by leaps and bounds. A national magazine for the Southern Baptist Sunday School Board even invited me to write several articles about the reasons my division was growing so rapidly. Our Sunday school had begun to see scores of people saved and discipled, and our denomination was very interested in the methods we were using to achieve that measure of success so quickly.

Every Monday morning, the pastor held a pastoral staff meeting in his office. I could hardly wait to go there each week so I could share all my glowing reports of what God was doing in our Sunday school division. I would sit there quietly, listening as the other pastors shared about their own areas of ministry, and I'd think to myself, *If I were you and that was all I had to share, I would be embarrassed!* I knew that my division was far exceeding theirs!

One Monday morning, I waited for my turn to share with my usual critical, impatient attitude. When it was finally time for me to speak, I reported with great exultation all of the wonderful things that were happening in my division. When I was finished, I looked at my beloved mentor, fully expecting him to say, *That's wonderful, Rick! You are the greatest, most inspiring member of our team! We're so grateful God has given you to us. Where would we be without you?*

Instead, my pastor looked sternly at me, reached down, took off one of his expensive shoes, and said, "Rick, I scuffed my shoes this morning as I was walking out of the house. I want you to take them to the shoe-repair shop right now and have them repaired. The rest of the pastors will stay here and continue our meeting — but as for you, I want you to go get my shoes buffed."

"Here are my car keys," the pastor continued. "You can drive my car over to the shoe shop. And while you're out in my car, please wash, wax, buff, and vacuum it before you bring it back. Then when you return, I'll have another assignment for you."

I'll never forget how devastated I felt that day. Instead of hearing this man tell me, "Great job!" — I heard nothing about what I had accomplished in my Sunday school division. In fact, he seemed to ignore what I'd shared altogether! As I walked out of his office, I thought, *What an ingrate! I'm working my fingers to the bone day and night, and all he can say is, "Now go shine my shoes." He didn't even say, "Thank you"!*

That day I did what every associate or assistant is tempted to do from time to time regarding the leader he or she serves: *I picked up an offense.* When a person takes an offense, he suddenly begins to see things differently. Because I was offended, it didn't take too long for me to see what I wanted to see. Previously, the pastor I worked with was, in my mind, the most anointed man on earth. But after that incident, I began to see him as selfish and self-centered. Day by day my offense grew larger until I even began to think, *If only the rest of the church could see what I see and know the pastor the way I know him, they wouldn't be so thrilled with him anymore!*

The truth is, there *were* some minor flaws in my pastor's life, but they were *very* minor. Of course, there are minor flaws in every person's life. Everyone has blind spots that he or she can't see.

There *were* times when my pastor could have been more loving — but then again, so could I. There were times when he could have been more grateful, but so could I. And there were times when he appeared insensitive, but these instances were very, very rare.

But because I was offended, my pastor's minor, insignificant flaws seemed huge to me. My offense completely colored my opinion of this man and began to tarnish a relationship that God desired to be close and beneficial to my training and spiritual growth. I began to think, *Well, if I were the pastor, I'd do things differently. If I were the pastor, I'd be more loving. If I were the pastor...*

In reality, my mentor was a man of integrity and good character, but my offended flesh was temporarily blinded to his wonderful attributes. Because I held on to my offense, all of his negative traits were magnified in my imagination to an abnormal degree.

My attitude toward this pastor was very wrong — but as I look back on this situation today, I actually thank God it happened! God used this precious man to expose serious character flaws in me that needed to be dealt with. At the time I thought I was very modest and humble — but my pride and arrogance were exposed through this man's careful handling of me. The pastor knew that pride had to be broken and removed from my life if I was going to be used in a significant way in the future.

The pastor was wise to have me shine his shoes and wash his car in the midst of my "great" achievements. My ugly reaction to his requirements exposed something in me that I didn't know was there, eventually bringing me to the realization that I needed to purify the motivations of my heart and the thoughts in my mind. Thank God for that pastor's insight into my life! What he required from me was just what I needed, even though I thought it was so unfair at the time!

Looking back on that experience, I'm so grateful to God for allowing me to learn under such a wise, godly man. Yes, he had minor flaws, but who doesn't? The real problem was my own immaturity. I was young and inexperienced, and I desperately wanted to be respected and viewed as an equal. But in truth, I wasn't an equal to this man in any way, shape, or form. I was just beginning my pilgrimage, but he had walked intimately with God for many years.

Eventually as I grew older, I repented for my youthful arrogance, and today I have a precious relationship with this man. He and I became close friends. After that time of offense had passed, I began to realize what I've been sharing in this book — that all leaders have flaws and idiosyncrasies and that they're actually no different from the rest of us. Although they're called to lead, they're still normal human beings who need the Lord's help to grow and change.

If you're serving under a mighty yet flawed man of God whose imperfections have disappointed or offended you in some way, you have two options available to you. You can hold on to your offense and stand in judgment of him — thus causing a great and possibly insurmountable hindrance to the fulfillment of your calling. *Or* you can allow God to mature you by forgiving your leader, remaining faithful and obedient to him, and working on your own flaws that regularly trip you up in your spiritual walk (*see* Hebrews 12:1).

> **In every situation, you are always given a choice as to how you will respond.**

In every situation, you are always given a choice as to how you will respond.

FAITHFUL IN THE TIME
OF PREPARATION

As I stated earlier, it is clear to me that Joshua must have passed this same kind of leadership test. How do I know? Well, let me ask you again: *What do you think it would have been like to work for Moses?*

As we've already seen, Moses didn't like to delegate authority to others, and he was impatient to the point of throwing a temper tantrum in the sight of God. If Moses lost his temper with God, we can be sure that he also lost his temper with people at times.

Furthermore, if Moses' judgment was ever questioned, he could always truthfully say that he was the only man to speak to God face to face and that he knew more about God and His ways than anyone else. His response to someone who questioned him may have sometimes been accompanied with the attitude, *Who are you to question me?*

Moses could truthfully say that God had used *him* to bring plagues on Egypt, part the Red Sea, destroy Pharaoh's army, and deliver the Ten Commandments to the children of Israel. *Can you imagine working for a man with all those credentials?* What could young Joshua ever tell the spokesman of God that he didn't already know? If anyone was a know-it-all, it would have been Moses.

Yet through the years, Joshua refused to budge from his God-called place beside Moses. He served faithfully through every kind of problem, including rebellions and insubordination, negativism and evil reports, disagreements, and even temper tantrums. No matter what, Joshua continued to be faithful, assisting his leader in any way that was required.

Joshua passed the leadership test! He could have become disillusioned with the flaws he saw in Moses' life and left the faith altogether. He could have been bitterly disappointed that the man of God wasn't always perfect. He could have even tried to overthrow Moses. But Joshua did none of these things.

As a result, God didn't reach for a newcomer to fill the gaping leadership hole that Moses left when he died. Instead, He personally elected Joshua to a position of great responsibility. God knew that because Joshua had learned to submit to a challenging man, he would be able to submit to an invisible God and do whatever was required of him.

If you want to be used by God in a leadership capacity, don't despise where you are right now.

What you're doing right now may seem small and insignificant. Yet the right actions, attitudes, and faithfulness you're cultivating in this present season will become the foundation of your future usefulness to God. Jesus said that if you were faithful over the little things, then He would give you rule over much (*see* Matthew 25:21).

If you're serving in a subordinate position in a church, organization, or business, you may feel like you're not being fully appreciated, even though you're doing exactly what you've been told to do. If that's the case, make a firm determination to be patient and to keep doing the very best you can to fulfill your present assignment with excellence. In the long run, you'll look back at this time and recognize how much God was working in you "...both to will and to do of his good pleasure" (Philippians 2:13).

When God works good things *into* you, He is simultaneously weeding *out* your wrong motivations and character flaws. This is an important time in your life — so don't despise the experience! Someday, you'll thank God for every moment of it.

A word of caution, though: If you find you have a critical spirit toward those in leadership over you, you're not yet ready for a leadership mantle yourself. If your expectations of other leaders are beyond reason, you need to realize that God uses real people just like you. Don't let their humanity send you into a tailspin of disillusionment or despair!

If you show mercy now, someday when you're placed in a greater leadership position, people will show mercy to you in spite of your failures and flaws.

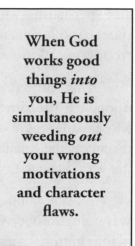

When God works good things *into* you, He is simultaneously weeding *out* your wrong motivations and character flaws.

DON'T WASTE TIME!

After all those years of dreaming what it would be like to be the leader of the Israelites, the spotlight finally shifted to Joshua in a moment's time. Joshua became the new Moses! Emotionally, he must have felt slightly panicked inside, thinking, *It's finally happened! It's here! It's no longer a dream! What do I do? I'm the new Moses!*

I can guess what Joshua wished he could do. He probably wished he could go talk to Moses and get a little advice! But an afternoon session with Moses to discuss and mull over a few ideas was an impossible dream. Joshua's mentor was dead, and all the responsibility of leading the Israelites was now resting on his shoulders.

As Joshua stood before the children of Israel for the first time as their new leader, they were naturally comparing him to Moses and speculating whether or not he would be able to fill Moses' shoes. And Joshua was more than likely looking back at them and wondering, *Will I ever be able to handle this job?*

All of Joshua's years of experience were about to be called upon. All the time he had spent training for this moment at Moses' side was about to be put into action. It seems that in one moment, the finality of Moses' death truly sunk in, and Joshua's life was changed.

God was calling Joshua to a new place of commitment. If he was going to obey God and take on the assignment God had set before him, it would require him to put aside his fears, questions, doubts, and insecurities in order to move into a higher realm of faith and courage.

Your time will also come! Right now, the Holy Spirit may have you in training for future leadership or a position of greater responsibility and influence. All of your past experiences and all the time and energy you're exerting in the present will eventually be called upon to help equip you for your future. Don't take this time in your life lightly!

If you're serving a pastor, an employer, or another type of leader, serve him or her with all of your heart. Fulfill your responsibilities as best as you can, and let God show you areas of your own heart that need to be changed. If you let the Holy Spirit deal with you now, it will spare you sorrow upon sorrow later down the road when it's time for *you* to become a leader or move into a position of greater responsibility.

If you're faithful to the call of God upon your life, the day will come when you will see the fullness of the vision He has given you come to pass. Suddenly all of your dreams will begin to come to fruition, and you'll have the rock-solid knowledge that things will never be as they once were.

Then after firmly dealing with all your fears, doubts, and questions, you will push yourself beyond the line God has asked you to cross with both trepidation and exultation — knowing with certainty that He has chosen you, molded you, and prepared you to be the person He needs for the task set before you. *That's the moment you will pass the point of no return.*

Think About It

An effective leader doesn't earn that description by chance. True leaders are cultivated one choice at a time. Gifting alone is not enough; integrity is a true leader's sustaining force. Distinctive qualities mark those who are qualified for leadership. Humility and faithfulness are bedrock qualities that are developed from the core of one's character, not drawn from charisma.

Do your habits and patterns of behavior reflect consistent, stable behavior? If so, what can you do to further strengthen those traits? If not, what do you need to adjust or completely change in order to sustain the full measure of leadership God has appointed you to carry?

❧

The ability to submit to authority is crucial, because only those who know how to follow are fully equipped to lead. Submission is not synonymous to agreement. Rather, it is the decision to remain subordinate to the person in authority, regardless of one's own preference or opinions. A submissive heart is focused on fulfilling the assignment given. And although it doesn't bow to abuse, neither does it yield to the temptation to judge the flaws or imperfections of the one in authority.

As you honestly review your journey leading to this present moment, do you recall moments when your own pride, stubbornness, or selfish ambition hindered you from being faithful to those in authority over you? How did you navigate those stumbling blocks, and what was the outcome? What is your plan to avoid being tripped up or disqualified by those attitudes in the future?

CHAPTER FOUR

FOCUSING ON YOUR FUTURE

*M*any times Christians who are called to begin a big, new assignment pin their hopes on receiving a powerful word from the Lord to kick off the next phase of their lives with a supernatural bang! They fantasize about receiving a prophecy that might go something like this: *"Thus sayeth the Lord, I have called and anointed you to take My Word to the nations!"*

Inwardly these believers long to hear God tell them, *"I will do wonderful and earth-shaking things through you as you take on this big assignment."* To them this kind of prophetic utterance would be the "green light" they needed to rest assured that they will have amazing, unprecedented success in all of their endeavors.

However, expecting God to give you this kind of prophetic word isn't realistic. For example, if you look at the life of Joshua, you'll see that he didn't receive that kind of word when it was time for him to assume *his* new role. He *did* receive a word from the Lord, but it wasn't an incredibly encouraging, flowery prophecy. Rather, it was straight to the point and hard to hear, and it probably struck him like a slap in the face.

God started out by saying, *"MOSES MY SERVANT IS DEAD..."* (Joshua 1:2). What a way for Joshua to start his ministry! Then God continued, "...Now therefore arise, go over this

Jordan, thou, and all this people, unto the land which I do give to them, even to the children of Israel."

When Joshua heard those fateful words, "Moses My servant is dead," it must have hit him really hard. But mourning for Moses wouldn't help or change the situation. Moses' role had already been fulfilled, and the next phase of God's plan was about to begin. It was time for Joshua to stop looking backward and start looking ahead. *It was time for Joshua to start focusing on his future.*

Have you ever come to a place in your life when you knew that your present season was ending and that it was time to move on — no matter how glorious or wonderful that season had been? If so, you learned a universal truth: When a phase of your spiritual walk is finished, it can never be extended or repeated. All you can do is move forward toward the next new assignment God gives you.

> **When a phase of your spiritual walk is finished, it can never be extended or repeated. All you can do is move forward toward the next new assignment God gives you.**

However, if God has put a dream in your heart that has yet to be fulfilled, you wouldn't want to stay forever where you are right now anyway! If you did, you'd never break into new territory and see that dream come to pass. You'd never know what it's like to throw your fears and apprehensions to the wind and fervently pursue God's perfect plan for your life!

Breaking free of your comfort zone to accept your new assignment — whether it's witnessing to your neighbor or moving across the world to preach the Gospel — will make you feel like you're living on the edge. It may be difficult at first. But after you've lived out on the edge for a while and grown accustomed to the daily adventure of serving Jesus Christ, you'll wonder how you were ever satisfied before you stepped out in faith. In retrospect, your former life will look boring and terribly uneventful compared to your new walk of obedience, which is filled with power and daily adventure as you watch to see what God will do through you.

Before God called Denise and me to take our ministry to the former Soviet Union, we both felt happy and fulfilled with our lives in the United States. As I discussed earlier, we had worked very hard to see our ministry grow and were seeing great success. When we thought back to how we had once pastored a little church in a small Arkansas town, we could see how much we'd grown in our faith to be able to cultivate a nationwide teaching ministry.

At the time, it seemed to Denise and me that we were already living on the edge. We never imagined that life could be more fulfilling or exciting. But from where we stand today, the challenges of our former traveling ministry pale in comparison to what we experience on a daily basis, living and ministering in the former USSR!

However, even though our itinerant teaching ministry was not God's ultimate plan for Denise and me, it was still a very important chapter in our spiritual walk. In fact, that period of our lives became the very foundation of our current ministry overseas. It was a necessary phase of spiritual growth and a time to develop important relationships that God is still using today. To have skipped that season of our ministry would have been like going from step one to step ten in God's plan for us and missing all the vital steps in between. We couldn't be where we are today if we hadn't taken all of the steps needed to get here. Only then could Denise and I begin our journey to take the Word of God to the uttermost parts of the earth.

When we arrived in the Soviet Union right before it collapsed, "living on the edge" took on a brand-new meaning to us. In the past, it had meant trying to pay the bills on time while we followed through with what God had asked us to do. But from that moment on, living on the edge began to mean much more. It still included paying all the bills — a challenge that had grown exponentially with the added expenses of living on the mission field. But we also had to navigate a very different culture with an entirely different set of rules and laws. Meanwhile, we endeavored to take God's Word to places where the Gospel had never yet been preached.

Through the years, our faith has grown to such a level that the new assignments God gives us no longer sound scary. In fact, they're thrilling! We feel like a team of race horses, eagerly awaiting our next "impossible" task from the Lord so we can enter the next phase of our spiritual race!

Paying the bills each month will always be a part of our responsibilities, just as it is for everyone. But now the dynamics have changed, and our perspective is drastically different. Our faith in God to provide has been firmly established, and our world vision has expanded. As one dear friend so aptly put it, "The world has become our playground, the place where God has called us to live and work!"

> **If Denise and I hadn't taken our many earlier steps of obedience, we would never be able to think big enough to embrace what God has shown us about the future.**

Today God is using our entire family to take the teaching of His Word to the United States, Europe, and the farthest ends of the former USSR. What will be next? Only God knows. Some things have been shown to us by the Holy Spirit, and it far surpasses anything we've ever done. But if Denise and I hadn't taken our many earlier steps of obedience, we would never be able to think big enough to embrace what God has shown us about the future. All these other steps, some little, some bigger, some gigantic, were necessary to prepare us for every next phase.

When we first began years ago, every step of faith initially terrified me. But frankly, we have now experienced the faithfulness of God and His awesome power so many times that every new step of faith is thrilling! And don't tell us that our next assignment from Heaven is impossible, because we're already doing what no one thought was possible!

What is *your* next great leap of faith? Is it:

- Leaving your current job to accept a new one with greater responsibilities?

- Starting a business that you've always dreamed of starting?

- Recognizing that you've finally met the woman or man God wants you to marry and then finally saying yes to that lifetime commitment?

- Pushing your fears aside to share Christ with your neighbor or unsaved family members?

- Stepping out in faith to answer God's call on your life to the ministry?

We're all at different phases and places in our lives. What's important is that we continue to move forward and focus on the future. We must not allow ourselves to get bogged down in life and lose the vision God has given us.

What are you going to do with your life? What is your next step? If you are stuck in a rut, are you going to stay where you are? Or are you going to break out of your stale status quo to embark on the great adventure God has planned for you?

TAKING THE BIG LEAP OF FAITH

If you're ready and willing to pursue the will of God for your life, you need to pay close attention to the next words God spoke to Joshua: "Moses my servant is dead: *now therefore arise...*" (Joshua 1:2). This is an extremely important statement because God emphatically told Joshua when to begin his assignment — he was to launch out *immediately*.

Perhaps you've received a clear word from the Lord calling you to begin a new assignment. However, instead of obediently follow His instructions, you're waiting for the circumstances to be absolutely perfect before you step out and obey. Well, let me tell you a sobering truth: *The situation will never be perfect!* Consider the life of Joshua. When God told him to lead the Israelites across the Jordan River, it was at flood stage. Believe me — that would be a very difficult way to start a ministry!

> **What are you going to do with your life? If you are stuck in a rut, are you going to stay where you are?**

Many believers like to say they're waiting for the perfect timing of the Lord before they make a move. But this is often nothing more than a poor excuse they use to avoid doing any real action.

Don't let this describe you! If God has instructed you to start your new assignment *now*, then *now* is His perfect timing! Don't be concerned if conditions don't seem fully conducive for launching into the new season. In fact, if conditions do seem perfect, you might need to reassess your situation and ask the Holy Spirit for discernment!

Perfect conditions don't necessarily mean perfect timing.

There comes a time in all of our lives when we no longer need to pray about the future — all we need to do is *act*. Joshua didn't need to stop and say, *Lord, let me pray about this new assignment for a few more days. I want to make sure the timing is absolutely perfect.* He had already spent decades training and praying for his opportunity. When his point of no return came, the only action required of him was *obedience*. That's why God simply said, "*...Now* therefore arise...."

Many Christians over-spiritualize their decisions, thinking they need to pray about the details just a little longer. But while they're praying, they miss out on the golden opportunity God has set in front of them. It was a *"now"* opportunity, and they missed it because they hesitated.

There's a time to pray, and there's a time to act. Sadly, many believers confuse the two and end up praying a lot without ever accomplishing anything with their lives. Therefore, it's vital to know when to quit praying and start acting.

Crucial to this understanding is being able to discern between the two different kinds of hesitation. The first kind is a hesitation in your spirit, which is the Holy Spirit telling you to slow down. The other kind of hesitation is your flesh not wanting to move forward into something new and unfamiliar. Most often, when you're feeling hesitant about pursuing your new assignment, you'll find that it's your flesh speaking to you rather than the Holy Spirit.

It's very important for you to know which voice you're hearing — that of your flesh or that of the Holy Spirit. If it's the voice of Holy Spirit, you'll have an unshakable, immovable warning on the inside, telling you to stop and pray. But if it's only your flesh trying to slow you down, you need to shove aside your fears and forge ahead to start your new God-given assignment.

This brings me to another very important point. If the opportunity before you is a door that you've kicked open yourself, you need to stop and pray to find out where the Holy Spirit really wants you to be. Young ministers, businessmen, and even volunteers in the church sometimes make the mistake of trying to promote themselves by manipulating their way into positions of authority. But this is always a recipe for disaster!

Let *God* promote you! Follow where He leads, and pass every test He sets before you with courage and faithfulness. If you promote yourself too soon, you won't be prepared to do the job, and you'll only set yourself up for failure. Remember, only God knows when you're ready for the door of opportunity to be opened to you, and only He knows what you'll need to succeed once you've stepped through.

> **Only God knows when you're ready for the door of opportunity to be opened to you, and only He knows what you'll need to succeed once you've stepped through.**

If the door you've been patiently waiting and praying for *supernaturally* opens and God gives you the green light, go for it! If you're nervous about taking that first step, don't worry. Those butterflies in your stomach are normal. You're about to step out in faith and do something you've never done before. Don't let your apprehension and nervousness keep you from achieving the wonderful things God has in store for your life. Those first steps of faith only look huge because you've never taken them before.

Once you've moved into the realm of faith to accept your new assignment from God, you'll realize that making that critical first move wasn't so difficult after all. But be careful to recognize that God is working on your behalf, and avoid over-spiritualizing your decision. That will only rob you of God's blessings when He tries to bring them to you.

Let me share an example from my own life. Many years ago our ministry began broadcasting our Christian television program throughout the former Soviet Union. One day as I was visiting with a television official who had once been a powerful leader in the fallen Communist regime, he looked at me and asked, "Rick, can you please provide us with a quality music television program for young people that has strong moral, Christian lyrics?"

I remember thinking to myself, *Should I pray about this before I answer?* But right then the answer came loud and clear to my spirit: *"When an incredible door of opportunity is opened to you by a lifelong atheist who wants you to provide Christian music for unsaved young people to hear — you don't stop to pray. You simply say, YES."*

Had I chosen to go home and pray about the question for several weeks, the door might have slammed shut before I ever responded. Who knows what would have happened in that time? By the next time I saw that Communist leader, his heart could have changed, and I would have lost an opportunity to take the Gospel to young people all over Russia. That was a *"now"* opportunity, and I'm so thankful that I recognized it. God was opening a door, and I accepted the challenge!

When you know God is calling you to accept a new assignment, it's incredibly important that you obey His leading. He has opened a new door of opportunity for you, and it's up to you to go ahead and walk through it! Ultimately, someone is going to do that job God has called you to do, so it may as well be you!

What opportunity is before you right now? Are circumstances lining up for you to fulfill the dream that has been in your heart? Do you sense a "green light" in your heart to move forward? If so, then go for it! This may be your *"now"* opportunity. Don't let it pass you by and leave you wondering what would have happened if you had taken the big leap of faith. *Have the courage to take the leap!*

Preparation, Not Perfection

In Joshua 1:2, God continued speaking to Joshua, saying, "Moses my servant is dead: now therefore *arise*...." I want you to notice that God told him to "arise."

This was Joshua's time to be promoted in the Kingdom of God. He couldn't hesitate, waver, or allow any of his own insecurities to stop him now. It was time for him to meet the challenge before him and move forward into God's plan for his life. It was time for Joshua to *ARISE*!

One translation renders the word "arise" as "prepare." This reveals that God uses believers who prepare — those who regularly seek to hear His voice through prayer and who daily seek to both understand and do the Word. They don't idly sit around, waiting for their ministry to begin. They learn all they can learn, soaking up everything the Holy Spirit teaches them, year after year after year.

Joshua was a man of preparation. He watched Moses, imitated Moses, and was discipled by Moses. He did all that was necessary to get himself ready for the moment when God would call upon him. Joshua's promotion did not happen overnight! He spent decades preparing for the time when he would become the leader of the nation of Israel.

I often hear believers say, "Wow! That person's ministry has really skyrocketed fast!" Or they may say, "Isn't it amazing how quickly his (or her) ministry has gained national prominence?" Yet if those same people were to really get to know the leaders they're talking about, they'd find out there is absolutely nothing "instant" about their success.

In fact, most of these ministers have been around a long, long time, working hard at their ministries for many years. It just so happens that they were promoted by God only recently and the fruit of their hard labors are finally being recognized. It's true that a few people achieve success quickly, but they often don't last very long because they aren't mature enough to *maintain* success.

This principle holds true in the business realm as well. A person may have been generally unknown until he was placed in a highly visible position. But just because no one knew who he was before that moment doesn't mean he wasn't working hard at the company all along. When he was finally promoted, people may have asked, "How in the world was that person given such a prominent position so quickly? Where did he come from anyway?" But in reality, it wasn't a quick promotion at all!

Promotion to a leadership position most often comes only after years of learning submission, faithfulness, and hard work. Normally the new leader who seemed to "step out of nowhere" into his role of authority actually came up through the ranks, putting in long hours over a long period of time. After years of diligence, he finally attained this position of influence and authority — and he earned it through the sweat of his brow.

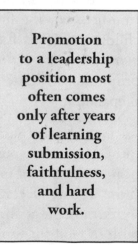

Promotion to a leadership position most often comes only after years of learning submission, faithfulness, and hard work.

To some of the Israelites, it may have seemed like Joshua stepped out of nowhere onto center stage. A few may have even thought he was an incredible overnight success story. But if you look closely at Joshua's life, you'll find that he had been around for a *long* time before he was promoted to a highly visible leadership position.

Forty years earlier, Moses had sent his first delegation of spies to search out the Promised Land, and Joshua was among them.

At that time, Joshua was generally unknown to the people of Israel, but Moses recognized Joshua's faithfulness. He knew that he could depend on Joshua to undertake that critical mission of espionage.

When that first delegation of spies returned home from the Promised Land, most of the group declared that the land was too difficult to take. Only Joshua and Caleb disagreed. Full of faith, Joshua declared, "If the Lord delight in us, then he will bring us into this land, and give it us..." (Numbers 14:8). Joshua had a spirit of faith, and he was willing to do whatever was necessary to accomplish the task in front of them.

Therefore, to say Joshua was an instant success would be a great misjudgment. As we've already seen, Joshua was a hard-working, faithful servant who had worked alongside Moses for several decades before the spotlight shifted to focus on him. Joshua's success only seemed sudden because he had been serving under the shadow of Moses. But when Moses died, that shadow vanished. For the first time in his life, Joshua stood before the children of Israel fully exposed. *He had been standing there the entire time, but his work had been hidden from public view.* His promotion to leadership came only after years of training and preparation.

Don't be discouraged if it takes a long time for you to move into a prominent position in your ministry or business or if you hear about tales of instant success. If you were to closely examine those instant-success stories, you'd find that in most cases, they weren't instant at all. It required a lot of work, sweat, prayer, and faith in God for those leaders to get where they are today. They started out in much the same way you did, and they had to face many of the same struggles that you may be facing right now.

A prominent, influential position isn't obtained only on the merit of one's gifts, talents, or abilities. Rather, it requires a stick-with-it attitude and a determination to keep going, even in the midst of difficult circumstances. Remember, Jesus had to face the Cross in order to experience the Resurrection!

TAKING JESUS AS OUR EXAMPLE

The Bible tells us to look at the life of Jesus and see what He endured to finish His race. Hebrews 12:2 says, "Looking unto Jesus the author and finisher of our faith; who for the joy that was set before him endured the cross, despising the shame, and is set down at the right hand of the throne of God."

Jesus is the Author and Finisher of our faith, and His walk of faith led Him to the Cross. However, this was a crucial phase of His faith walk, without which He could never have accomplished the assignment given to Him by God the Father. Jesus' purpose during His time on this earth was to redeem mankind — and in order to fulfill that purpose, He had to face death.

Jesus clearly didn't enjoy the Cross! Hebrews 12:2 says He "endured" the Cross and "despised" the shame. That word "endure" comes from the Greek word *hupomeno*. It's a compound of the words *hupo* and *meno*. The word *hupo* is a preposition that means *under*, and the word *meno* means *to abide* or *to stay*. When the two are compounded, the new word portrays *a person who is under some type of incredibly heavy load but who refuses to stray from his position because he is committed to his task*. Regardless of the load, opposition, stress, or weight that comes against him, he is *not* going to move. He is going to stay put in his spot and not surrender it to anyone for any reason. This describes Jesus' stance of faith as He set His face like flint toward the Cross, *despising* the shame.

That word "despise" comes from the Greek word *kataphroneo*, which means *to despise, to scorn, to disregard*, or *to show one's hatred for something by active insult*. That definition can't begin to convey how Jesus felt as He anticipated what would be required of Him in order to fulfill His divine assignment.

Would you want to be ridiculed, stripped naked, beaten horribly, scourged, and ultimately crucified before a crowd of mocking faces? Would you want to spend three days in the darkness of hell? *No, of course you wouldn't!*

Jesus didn't want to do undergo those torments either, but He endured them because He was focused on the future. He had His sights set on redeeming mankind and being seated at His Father's right hand. Jesus could have called on 12 legions of angels to deliver Him from the hands of His enemies (*see* Matthew 26:53). *That's 72,000 angels!* Jesus could have even said, "Father, I've decided that I don't want to go through with this," and God would have released Him from His assignment.

But because Jesus had His heart set on redeeming humanity, He endured unspeakable persecution and suffering, thus obtaining reconciliation between God and man through His death and resurrection. In the face of incredible opposition, Jesus accomplished what His Father had sent Him to do!

> During Jesus' life on earth, temporary creature comforts were never as important as the assignment He had been given by the Father.

During Jesus' life on earth, temporary creature comforts were never as important as the assignment He had been given by the Father. If it had been otherwise, He wouldn't have been born in a manger stall; He wouldn't have grown up in Nazareth; and He wouldn't have faced the Cross. Accomplishing what He had been sent to do was paramount in Jesus' heart and mind.

Likewise, you have to be absolutely committed to your assignment if you're going to become all that God wants you to be. Those who are more concerned about their creature comforts than achieving victory will eventually fall by the wayside and fail. But if you're willing to pay the price, you'll be standing tall when all of those pushovers are gone, and you'll win the prize! Your endurance and refusal to quit will prove that you're a mighty champion of faith.

On that day, you'll know better than anyone else the struggles you overcame. Although your faith may have gone through rocky times, you had the guts to stay in the fight. You never gave up or lost sight of your call. And as a result, people will see you as a spiritual giant!

A combination of courage, guts, and determination is a formula that always produces incredible leaders — people who stand taller than anyone else. Because they're willing to go the distance, their persevering attitude and drive eventually produce greatness in their lives.

LET YOUR ROOTS GROW DOWN DEEP
TO GIVE YOU A SURE STANDING

Long before a fruit-producing tree can blossom and bear fruit, it must first send its roots down deep into the earth to find nourishment. Only after the tree has begun to draw from a constant source of nourishment below does it begin to send its limbs upward and outward.

As the tree grows, it may endure heat, cold, sleet, rain, drought, and snow before it ever blossoms. Yet because its roots are tapped into a continuous source of strength, nourishment, and energy, the tree is able to weather the seasons year after year and then eventually produce fruit.

According to Psalm 1:3, if a person is rooted in God's Word, he's "...like a tree planted by the rivers of water, that bringeth forth his fruit in his season; his leaf also shall not wither; and whatsoever he doeth shall prosper."

If you're currently wondering how long it's going to take for *your* fruit-producing season to finally arrive, don't be discouraged. The bigger a tree is, the longer it takes for it to send its roots down deep enough into the earth to draw nourishment and give itself a firm footing against wind, weather, and pestilence.

Instead of getting discouraged, follow the apostle Paul's counsel in Colossians 2:7 (*TLB*): "Let your roots grow down deep into him and draw your nourishment from him. See that you keep on growing in the Lord, and become strong and vigorous in the truths you were taught." Use this period of waiting to send your roots down deep and tap into the strength of God's Word and the Holy Spirit. If your roots are securely fixed in Jesus Christ, you'll outlast every dry season, every foul climate, and every storm — and eventually, you'll enter into the fruit-producing season of your life, your ministry, your family, or your business.

Honestly, you should be grateful that your promotion hasn't come quickly. If it had, you may have taken a leadership position without first establishing deep roots and a sure foundation. And when you began to experience the difficulties that inevitably come with the responsibility of leadership, you would have crumbled under the pressure.

While you're waiting for the next step in God's plan for you to come to pass, use this time of preparation to put off the old man and put on the new man (*see* Colossians 3:9,10). Work on improving areas of your own personal life — such as your self-discipline, your finances, your weight, your relationships, and your behavior. Renew your mind with the Word of God (*see* Ephesians 4:23), and make sure your affections are set "...on things above, not on things on the earth" (Colossians 3:2). If you have all of these areas of your life in order, you'll be in good shape when the time comes for you to be promoted to a position of greater responsibility.

One of the saddest things I see on a regular basis is talented men and women who have been promoted too quickly and thus lack the spiritual roots and depth of character needed to sustain them. Unfortunately, this is all too common — even in the Body of Christ.

For instance, think about how many times you've heard about a celebrity or public figure who was saved and then began preaching within a few weeks or months of his or her salvation. These people often kick off their ministries with a big bang but then watch as their ministries end in a terrible fizzle. Whoever promoted them so quickly did them a great injustice. Instead of quickly gaining prominence within the Body of Christ, the new converts should have gotten involved in a local church where they could diligently hear and do the Word of God and be discipled. Then when they were spiritually mature, God Himself would speak to them, and they would be ready to be sent out.

Let your dreams for the future be your motivation in the present to straighten out your life and to grow and mature in your spiritual walk!

Let your dreams for the future be your motivation in the present to straighten out your life and to grow and mature in your spiritual walk!

Time To Prepare, Grow,
Change, and Become Trusted

The apostle Paul was a naturally talented and gifted man. Even before he was saved, he was well-known and respected in important Jewish circles. He was from the tribe of Benjamin, a member of the Sanhedrin, and a nationalistic extremist for the cause of Israel. And because of his education, he had become one of the greatest intellectual minds of his time.

Therefore, it shouldn't come as a surprise that when Paul accepted Jesus Christ as his Messiah, he thought he deserved to be promptly promoted to a position of leadership in the Christian community. Soon after Paul became a Christian, he traveled to the city of Jerusalem to join up with the disciples. But Paul was still so new to the faith that the disciples weren't even sure if he was really saved!

Concerning this interaction, Acts 9:26 and 27 recounts: "And when Saul [Paul] was come to Jerusalem, he assayed to join himself to the disciples: but they were all afraid of him, and believed not that he was a disciple. But Barnabas took him, and brought him to the apostles, and declared unto them how he had seen the Lord in the way, and that he had spoken to him, and how he had preached boldly at Damascus in the name of Jesus."

Barnabas believed Paul's testimony right from the start, but it took a bit of convincing for the other disciples to rest assured. Even after they knew with certainty that Paul's testimony was sincere, their response was cautious and measured. They didn't immediately send out advertisements saying that the world's greatest Christian-killer had been saved, nor did they immediately launch him into an itinerant ministry to reach the world for Jesus. They were wiser than that!

Instead, the disciples in Jerusalem put Paul on a ship and sent him back to his own hometown of Tarsus. Once there, Paul probably shared the news of his salvation with his family and took care of any personal business that needed attention. No one can say for sure what happened with Paul's family, but one thing is certain. His public ministry didn't begin until many years after his salvation experience.

That period of waiting served as a time of personal and spiritual growth for Paul. During those years, he served God and the members of the apostolic team in Antioch and began to develop godly character. Paul also studied the Bible intensely, gleaning new, incredible revelations about the Lord Jesus from the Old Testament.

Finally, after years of serving under other ministers, Paul was ready to be sent forth into the mission field for the very first time. Yet even then, he wasn't sent out alone. Rather, Paul was accompanied by Barnabas, who had first presented Paul to the disciples in Jerusalem and then subsequently became Paul's spiritual mentor.

It was for this reason that Paul later admonished Timothy to "lay hands suddenly on no man...." in order to avoid promoting an unprepared novice or a new believer to a position of leadership (1 Timothy 5:22). Likewise, this is why Paul required church elders and deacons to be men of character who had already proven their sincerity and stability in the local church before they were promoted into visible positions of leadership (*see* 1 Timothy 3:1-13). Paul was speaking from personal experience! He knew from his own spiritual walk that preparation, maturity, and experience are the keys to being successful in leadership.

Concerning himself, Paul told the Thessalonians, "But as we were allowed of God to be put in trust with the gospel, even so we speak; not as pleasing men, but God, which trieth our hearts"

(1 Thessalonians 2:4). I want you to notice the first part of this verse, which says, "But as we were *allowed* of God...."

This word "allowed" is the Greek word *dokimadzo*. Historically, this word was used to depict a man who had undergone many rigorous tests and trials to determine whether or not he had enough character to be placed in a position of leadership. If he couldn't pass these character tests, he was deemed unfit for public service and eliminated from consideration for that position.

Strength of character always takes precedent over gifts or talents.

Therefore, when Paul wrote, "But as we were *allowed* of God...," he was making a powerful statement about his own walk with the Lord. Rather than being thrust into a position of leadership too quickly after his new birth, Paul was put through a number of grueling character tests that proved he was fit for leadership in the Kingdom of God. Although Paul was called to the ministry, God wouldn't allow him to move into a visible position of leadership in the Body of Christ until his character had been developed, tested, and shown to be trustworthy.

> **Strength of character always takes precedent over gifts or talents.**

It's very likely that a big part of Paul's process of maturation involved learning to sit quietly and listen to the spiritually mature believers in Antioch — men who were perhaps less educated than himself, but nevertheless more knowledgeable and experienced in spiritual matters. In addition, he probably also had to learn humility by serving in unnoticed positions that he may have thought were far below his abilities or intelligence. Simply put — Paul had to learn be a brother like everyone else!

Promotion didn't come quickly for Paul. In fact, it took more than a decade! After he dealt with his flesh, pride, and strong will for more than a decade, Paul was deemed fit by God to enter into full-time ministry. Acts 13:2 records this long-awaited, landmark moment when the Holy Spirit spoke a prophetic word to the leaders in Antioch, saying, "...Separate me Barnabas and Saul [Paul] for the work whereunto I have called them."

Notice the Holy Spirit described the work of Paul and Barnabas as "...the work *whereunto I have called them*." Paul knew he was predestined for that assignment! No doubt he could vividly remember the prophecies that were spoken over him when he was first saved — prophecies that proclaimed him to be "...a chosen vessel unto me [God], to bear my name before the Gentiles and kings, and the children of Israel" (Acts 9:15).

From the very outset of his life in Christ, Paul knew that he had an important destiny and that he would play a major role in the Kingdom of God. Yet it took all those years of preparation before those prophetic words would begin to come to pass in his life. Before Paul could rise up as the great leader God intended him to be, the flaws in his character had to be exposed and then confronted by the leaders God had placed in authority over him.

At the end of those years of preparation, Paul was "...allowed of God to be put in trust with the gospel..." (1 Thessalonians 2:4). The phrase "to be put in trust" is translated from an old Greek phrase that means *to be put in public office, such as the office of mayor or governor*. By using this phrase, Paul was essentially saying, *"It took a long time, but after a series of hard trials and tests, God finally deemed me fit to be used by Him in a public capacity."* In other words, Paul passed his leadership test, and God saw him fit to be trusted in ministry.

However, Paul's promotion didn't mean he would never again face another test or trial in his life. Far from it! Paul concludes First Thessalonians 2:4 by saying, "...not as pleasing men, but God, which trieth our hearts." Because this statement in the

Greek is in present tense, Paul was essentially saying, *"After all the trials and tests I've been through in my past, God is still trying my heart today to make sure I remain fit for public service."*

God is always monitoring and reviewing our qualifications for leadership. He watches us closely to see how we respond to situations, how we walk in love toward people, how serious we are about the positions He has assigned to us, and how we handle His Word.

God is always monitoring and reviewing our qualifications for leadership.

Don't get discouraged if it takes time for your dream to become a reality in your life. God is never in a hurry because godly character is more far important to Him than gifts, talents, or worldly achievements.

You need to use your time right now to prepare, to change, and to grow so that when your time comes and you're finally promoted to a visible position of leadership, you'll have what you need internally and spiritually to fulfill your God-given assignment.

YOUR ULTIMATE GUARANTEE FOR A VICTORIOUS FUTURE

The Bible provides us with a key to ensure that our time of leadership will be fruitful and lasting. In Second Peter 1:5-7, Peter wrote, "And beside this, giving all diligence, add to your faith virtue; and to virtue knowledge; and to knowledge temperance; and to temperance patience; and to patience godliness; and to godliness brotherly kindness; and to brotherly kindness charity." Then in verse 8, Peter continued with a glorious promise, saying, "For if these things be in you, and abound, they make you that ye shall neither be barren nor unfruitful in the knowledge of our Lord Jesus Christ."

What a promise! If the qualities found in Peter's list abound in your life, then your endeavors will never be barren or unfruitful! However, there's a catch — it takes time and effort to develop all of those character traits. That's why Peter begins by saying, "...*giving all diligence....*" Developing those wonderful attributes in your life will require great diligence and tremendous commitment on your part.

It's important to make wise use of your time by sending your roots down deep into the character of Christ to develop faith, virtue, knowledge, temperance, patience, godliness, brotherly kindness, and charity. These qualities won't be cultivated overnight. To make them a reality in your life, you'll have to be committed to developing your character over a long period of time. But if you buckle down and apply yourself, the rewards will be immense.

As we saw earlier, God's decision to promote Joshua into a position of prominence wasn't based on a quick overnight decision. God had been examining Joshua's life for many years, looking for faithfulness, courage, character, strong moral values, and right responses to varied and difficult situations. He had been searching for someone with enough character to carry the kind of great anointing that Israel's leader would need — someone who was committed enough to step into that position of leadership and maintain it without becoming morally shipwrecked.

During Joshua's years of waiting, God gave him ample time to send his roots down deep. And because Joshua had time to grow and prepare, he was strong enough to weather any storm he might face when the time came for him to lead.

WHAT HAPPENED
TO THE OTHER TEN SPIES?

I've often wondered what happened to the other ten spies who went to check out the Promised Land with Joshua and Caleb but came back with a negative report. What did they do with their lives? What did they accomplish? How did they die?

> **Because Joshua had time to grow and prepare, he was strong enough to weather any storm he might face when the time came for him to lead.**

When these spies first set off to scope out the Promised Land, each of them had the same potential as Joshua. If they hadn't, Moses wouldn't have sent them out and entrusted them with such a dangerous mission. They were Joshua's contemporaries, associates, and peers.

But although the other ten men also had the potential to become great leaders, they were eliminated from God's plan because they limited their faith and thinking. Instead of moving forward into the Promised Land, they died in the wilderness, probably very regretful of the poor choices they made when they were younger. In the end, each amounted to nothing more than an unknown has-been from a previous generation.

Like these ten spies, people who miss their opportunities in life usually become critical and bitter toward others. Rather than rejoice when a leader succeeds, they nit-pick about everything the successful leader says or does. Always complaining, they spew forth a constant stream of negativity, saying things like, "That leader doesn't know what he's talking about," or, "If I were the leader, I'd do things differently."

But the truth is, these people don't stand in the position of responsibility that the leader does, and they should keep their negative thinking to themselves. It's their fault that they are where they are today, and if they want their *situation* to change, then *they* must change. Other people aren't their problem — *they* are their own problem.

There is nothing more grievous than seeing someone who once had great opportunity and potential become hardhearted, bitter, and cynical. What a waste of life!

Joshua's attitude made all the difference in his life, setting him apart at a young age as one possessing great potential for leadership. He was willing to go the extra mile, lay down his life, and serve for years without recognition under the leadership of Moses. As a result, when all the other spies were left behind to die as old men in the wilderness, Joshua remained pliable in the hands of God and was therefore able to be used in a powerful way.

Cynical Christians are usually people who once had great promise but then fell behind because of wrong decisions they made based on their own pride or unbelief. The only people who move forward toward their dreams are those who have been diligent and faithful to submit to authority in every position that God has placed them.

Like Joshua, believers who have a humble, pliable spirit always strive to submit to God's authority, no matter how difficult, challenging, impossible, tedious, or frustrating the process might seem at the time.

WHEN YOUR NEW ASSIGNMENT SEEMS IMPOSSIBLE

Going back to Joshua 1:2, we see that God continued to deliver his message to Joshua by saying, "Moses my servant is dead: now therefore arise, *go over this Jordan....*" Immediately after Joshua was called into ministry, he received his first assignment: *Lead the children of Israel across the Jordan River into the Promised Land.*

At that particular time, the Jordan River was at flood stage. Its raging waters were overflowing from its banks, and its currents were dangerously wild. Because Joshua's promotion was still so new, the Israelites were probably wondering if he had any leadership ability. So when Joshua told them that they were going to cross a large, flooding river, they probably thought that their doubts about him were right after all!

I can almost hear them saying, "Lead us across the Jordan at this time? Don't you realize that the river is at flood stage right now? Where is your mind? Do you intend to tell us that God actually told you to lead us over that river at this exact time? What kind of God would tell you to do such a crazy thing? That isn't even logical, Joshua!"

It wasn't as if the children of Israel were strangers to great demonstrations of God's power. Under the leadership of Moses, they had witnessed the Red Sea miraculously part at their feet so they could walk across a dry sea bed to the other side. But that, of course, was when Moses was the leader — *not Joshua.* In the minds of the Israelites, there was surely no way that Joshua could ever be the kind of leader that Moses had been!

This is precisely the reason that God initiated Joshua's ministry with a supernatural challenge. Something supernatural had to happen to prove to the people of Israel that Joshua really was God's man.

Place yourself in Joshua's shoes. How do you think he felt when he heard the Holy Spirit tell him to cross over the Jordan River? He knew the river was at flood stage and that he would probably receive a lot of criticism from some people for suggesting such a ridiculous idea. Beginning his ministry with this assignment would be an incredible leap of faith.

Joshua would have probably preferred to start out with a much simpler command from God, such as teaching people to pray or believing God to heal the sick. But that wasn't God's plan. Instead, God laid before Joshua an awesome task: *To lead millions of people across a flooding river that they didn't want to cross during the worst season of the year.*

When God first calls men or women into a position of leadership, sometimes He doesn't give them the leisure of taking tiny baby steps to ease their transition into their new roles. Instead, He requires them to do something monumental right at the start because their new assignments are so important. In these cases, God's intention is to show these new leaders that the Holy Spirit is always with them, as well as to prove to their followers that these men and women have what it takes to lead.

After the Jordan River parted and the Israelites passed through on dry ground, no one — including Joshua — ever questioned Joshua's anointing again. That supernatural intervention of God validated his ministry in the eyes of the entire nation.

There is a negativism in human nature that often causes people to sit back and watch someone take a step of faith while speculating about that person's potential failure. They may verbally express support to that person, but inwardly they often harbor unspoken reservations.

People like to hang back and watch for your next move. If your step of faith fails or if you don't follow through on your commitment, they may conclude that you can't really hear the voice of God or that your vision was bigger than your faith. But if they actually see you follow through on your words and accomplish something truly noteworthy that bears great fruit for God's Kingdom, you'll win over their hearts. And the next time you announce you're going to do something that sounds outrageous and wild to the natural mind, people will be much more inclined to believe you!

This kind of confidence was especially important for Joshua because he would lead the children of Israel into many seemingly outrageous situations over the course of his ministry. For instance, on multiple occasions, he led the people of Israel into battles where they were grossly outnumbered by their enemies. At such a numerical disadvantage, the Israelite fighters should have been slaughtered according to the natural — but they weren't. They won decisive victories over their enemies with the help of Almighty God!

The parting of the Jordan River not only established the people's confidence in Joshua's leadership, but it also built Joshua's confidence. When those waters parted, a new surge of supernatural faith doubtlessly rose up in Joshua's heart as he realized, *It's true! God really is with me! The same kind of anointing that was on Moses is now on me! I can see it!*

The miraculous event that transpired at the Jordan River was only the beginning, setting the stage for many other incredible signs and wonders to be wrought through Joshua. Later on in his ministry, Joshua would even command the sun to stand still, and it would remain still for an entire day. *Who would have ever thought such a thing would be possible?* Yet the parting of the Jordan River had proved once again that with God, nothing is impossible. Just as Joshua was able to command the waters to part, he could have commanded the sun to obey in order to fulfill the plan of God (*see* Joshua 10:12,13).

So don't be afraid to accept the new assignment that God has given to *you*. The task before you may look large, overwhelming, and even outrageous to your natural mind. But you can rest assured that if God has called you to do something, He has also equipped and anointed you to fulfill that assignment.

When the waters part before you and you pass through your predicament unharmed, you'll be left with a wonderful new confidence — an assurance that you're right in the middle of God's will for your life. *There is no greater confidence than knowing you're exactly where God wants you to be.*

> **You can rest assured that if God has called you to do something, He has also equipped and anointed you to fulfill that assignment.**

DON'T SIT ON THE BANKS

The worst thing you can do when you're faced with your own point of no return is to sit idly on the banks of your "Jordan River" and wonder, *Would it really part for me if I take this step of faith?*

Sadly, that is what most Christians do. Instead of believing God and taking action to see their dreams come to pass, they often just sit back and wait, obsessing about whether or not they should step out in faith and obey God. They watch from the sidelines as other believers take great leaps of faith. They may even read biographies of men and women who achieved greatness because they acted on a word from God to do the impossible. But when it comes to their own lives, they remain utterly immobile.

These Christians think and think about all the possible implications of what God is asking them to do until they finally realize they've missed their opportunity. Then when their time has passed, they wonder why their lives are devoid of excitement, adventure, and purpose! Too often people who fit in this category ultimately do nothing significant for God's Kingdom with their lives.

Friend, I'll tell you where adventure and excitement lie — *on the other side of the river*! The adventure begins when you focus on your future and start moving! When you first step off the bank and put your foot into the waters, you'll experience a surge of faith and excitement like you've never before known in your life. And when those waters part for you, you'll know a dimension of faith that can only be known by the bravest and most daring men and women of God.

Let me relate an example from own life. Years ago, I knew a young man who had great potential but was hindered from releasing that potential by fear and insecurity. He was a meticulous thinker, planner, and organizer — all wonderful qualities in their own right. However, he continually allowed excessive thinking and unnecessary planning to interfere with his ability to take a step of faith. God intended these qualities to be beneficial to this young man. Instead, he allowed these personality traits to build a stronghold in his mind that held him back from pursuing God's will for his life.

Opportunity after opportunity presented itself to this man. But instead of taking action, he would think so long about whether or not he should accept the new opportunity that it would just pass him by. Time after time, I watched as he sat back instead of moving forward, obsessively thinking and plotting his next move.

Finally, I said to him, "You need to recognize what God is doing when He is opening a door for you. When He gives you a green light, you need to obey what the Holy Spirit is telling you to do. Quit allowing your mind and your fears to prevent you from stepping out from where you are to where God wants you to be."

Sadly, this man continued to sit idly on the banks, looking at the wild river and wondering what would happen if he were to step out in faith to accept the new opportunity God had placed before him. The chains that bound the man weren't made of iron, but they were just as real. He had placed those chains on himself, and the longer he sat there, wondering without taking action, the stronger those chains became.

Don't let this be you! If you've been preparing for your moment of promotion and you sense that God is giving you the green light, take that first step off the banks of your Jordan River, and watch what God Almighty will do for you when you put your trust in Him! When those waters begin to part, you'll enter an amazing new realm of living from which there is no return. And I promise you — once you experience the excitement and fulfillment of pursuing the dream God has planted in your heart, you'll never *want* to go back to where you once were.

> Once you experience the excitement and fulfillment of pursuing the dream God has planted in your heart, you'll never want to go back to where you once were.

In addition, you'll have the faith, courage, and perseverance to boldly step into the next river when it presents itself — as well as the next and the next. With each new experience, God's faithfulness will build such a strong foundation of confidence in your heart that you'll be able to face every challenge on the road ahead with boldness and assurance.

So what is God telling you to do? Whatever it is, don't allow fear to stop you dead in your tracks. Refuse to let yourself get bogged down and lose the vision God gave you.

If you're certain God has spoken to you and you know what you're supposed to do right now, take the first step forward into your future! The waters in front of you may look wild and dangerous, but God will make a way for you to cross unscathed. Instead of focusing on all the problems and impossibilities in front of you, make the choice to push all those doubts aside and start focusing in faith on your future.

It's true that you should be realistic about your own talents, gifts, and finances, as well as about the problems you're facing. And if your problems are a result of your own actions or inaction, you need to set everything right before you step out to take another big leap of faith.

However, if you've taken the time to send your roots down deep into Christ; if your personal life is in order; and if you sense the Holy Spirit telling you that your time has come — *you've reached your point of no return.* Challenge, conquest, and victory lay before you. The realm of life you're about to enter is more satisfying than anything money could ever buy and more gratifying than any transient feeling of security could ever afford you.

Nothing can compare to following God's will for your life.

God Wants To Give You Something Wonderful!

In Joshua 1:2, God continued to speak to Joshua, saying, "Moses my servant is dead; now therefore arise, go over this Jordan, thou, and all this people, *unto the land which I do give to them,* even to the children of Israel."

I want you to especially notice that God said, *"...unto the land which I do give to them...."* The Promised Land was just beyond the Jordan River, and the Israelites were nearly there! For many years, they had heard about the Promised Land, continually hoping and praying that one day they would finally see it.

On their long, arduous journey to the land God had prepared for them, the children of Israel had endured all kinds of hardship. They had dealt with rebellions, famines, the scorching heat of the desert, poisonous snakes, and long years of wandering back and forth on the same trails. To top it all off, their beloved leader had died before they ever made it to the Promised Land, even though he was originally supposed to lead them there. What an intense journey they had endured!

However, through all of the trials and temptations this younger generation of Israelites had faced, many of them had held fast to the vision God had given them for a better life in a new land, just as Joshua had. They held personal dreams in their hearts that they wanted to fulfill in the new land — and dreams have power. Dreams sustain the fire for the larger vision, which people need in order to keep going when times become difficult.

The older generation always remembered the provision of Egypt, which is why they kept looking back again and again. But the younger generation had been born and raised in the desert and had never known life outside of that dusty, barren place. The idea of a clean, beautiful green land that flowed with milk and honey must have been an incredible dream for these young Israelites! Now as they stood on the banks of the Jordan, they could look across and see the land they had dreamed about their entire lives.

As younger Israelites stood there on the banks of the Jordan, God commanded Joshua to "...arise, go over this Jordan, thou, and all this people, unto the land which I do give to them, even to the children of Israel" (Joshua 1:2). Imagine how exciting that prophetic word must have been to those who had been waiting their whole lives for this moment! The dream was happening! The vision their parents had imparted to them was unfolding right before their eyes!

You and God Are Partners in Fulfilling Your Future

But what the Lord said next was crucial for the Israelites to understand if that vision was to be fulfilled. He went on to say, "Every place that the sole of your foot shall tread upon, that have I given unto you, as I said unto Moses" (v. 3).

God was promising His people, *"I'm giving you the land! Every place you put the sole of your foot upon is YOURS."* But notice that this was not an unconditional, unlimited promise. God would give the children of Israel the land, but they had to do their part.

In other words, God was telling them, *"As long as you sit on this side of the Jordan River and simply look at the Promised Land, it isn't yours and never will be! However, if you will cross the river and put your foot on the opposite bank, I'll give that particular piece of land to you. As you move ahead and place your feet on additional land, I'll give that to you as well. Every place that the soles of your feet touch will become yours."*

That same principle holds true for us regarding our inheritance as children of God through Christ. The only thing that is totally free in this world is God's grace. Grace for salvation, grace for the infilling of the Holy Spirit, grace for deliverance, grace to empower you to witness, grace to sanctify you, and grace to heal you — all of these come to you directly from God as His free gift to you!

But if you are going to be saved, *you* must pray. If you desire to be delivered, *you* must take action to be delivered. If you wish to become a witness, *you* must open your mouth and speak. If you want the Holy Spirit to sanctify you, *you* must have the desire to live a pure and holy life. If God is going to heal you, *you* must use your faith to receive it. God freely gives all of these wonderful gifts, but your actions, your attitude, and your faith are directly involved in receiving them.

Likewise, if you're going to see the vision God gave you come to pass in your life, *you* are going to have to get involved to make it happen. God will provide the grace you need to achieve it, but *you* must be God's partner in accomplishing your vision.

When the Lord first told Denise and me to begin our traveling teaching ministry so many years ago, we were so inspired to believe this promise of God. We started praying about our new assignment, asking the Holy Spirit to show us how to book more meetings. One day we sensed a leading to take our great big map of the United States off the wall and lay it on the floor. Then we began to walk across the states God was speaking to us about, proclaiming that every place we stepped on was ours!

This may have looked crazy to others, but to Denise and me, it was serious business! And do you know what? God honored our craziness! As we traveled throughout the nation during those years of itinerant ministry, we continued to repeat that declaration of faith again and again — and it wasn't long before we were receiving all kinds of calls from churches in all the states we had walked upon on our map!

> **God does everything in steps, but you and I are the ones who must take those steps to the destiny He has planned for us.**

God does everything in steps, but you and I are the ones who must take those steps to the destiny He has planned for us.

In order for Joshua and the people of Israel to receive God's promise, they had to get up and do some walking. As long as they just sat on the banks of the Jordan River, wondering what to do and fretting over the future, they would never get closer to the place He wanted them to be.

The children of Israel already knew the will of God. Now it was time for them to get up and act like they believed that His promise was true.

THINK ABOUT IT

Have you ever longed for change but surprisingly found yourself fighting to cling to your comfort zone when the time came for you to step out of the familiar and into the unknown? Ultimately, you will face a moment in your journey when what has been is no longer an option. Whether by choice or by force, you must move on.

Ignoring the future will not prevent it from overtaking you — hence, the value of quiet, focused preparation. What plan do you have in place to be prepared for the moment when "tomorrow" becomes your "today"? Have you asked God to prepare you for the destiny He has planned for you?

❧

Your preparation strategy today will help you recognize your custom-made opportunity tomorrow — even if that opportunity is something not necessarily preferred or expected.

Even more important than knowing and developing your strengths is to be able to identify and then fortify your weaknesses. Devote time and effort to strengthening the vulnerable areas in your character where you find yourself repeatedly susceptible to self-sabotage.

Monitor your own maturity level. If your gifts and potential opened a door to leadership for you now, would you be qualified to occupy that room? Are you diligent in matters big and small? Have you cultivated patience? Are you temperate and self-controlled in your personality and your appetites? Will your love walk sustain the level of faith you need to function as a leader? After you review your present qualifications, you may find that you need to focus less on looking for an opportunity and more on growing into a position of readiness when that opportunity comes into view.

CHAPTER FIVE

FIVE PRIMARY REASONS PEOPLE FAIL IN LIFE

*T*here are many reasons people choose to stay on "the banks of the river" and never venture out into an exciting new walk of obedience, faith, and power. In my book, *Dream Thieves*, I discuss hindrances that come against your dream from outside sources. I also briefly touch on one that is far more personal — you! It is this area that I want to discuss in more detail in this chapter.

Through my own experience and the many conversations I've had with other believers, I've found there are five primary vices that hinder people from getting up and doing something valuable with their lives. Of course, there are actually many more, but these particular five hindrances are universal to every human being and very closely related to each other. When one hindrance is present in a person's life, it's probable that some — if not all — of the others are present as well.

Just one of these roadblocks can prevent you from moving forward into the future God has designed for you. Therefore, it's imperative that you identify these hindrances if they're causing problems in your life and then rid yourself of them through the sanctifying power of the Holy Spirit. Otherwise, you'll find it very difficult, if not impossible, to fulfill the assignment God wants to give you.

These five primary hindrances are *laziness, unrealistic fantasies, slothfulness, creature comforts,* and *believing a bad report.* All believers have dealt with these issues to one degree or another at some point in their lives, so if you feel like the next few pages describe you, don't get under condemnation! Just allow the Holy Spirit to show you how to remove these stumbling blocks from your life, and diligently stick to His plan so you stay free forever. Left unchecked, any of these five vices has the power to knock you out of the game!

Reason Number One: Laziness

The Bible has a lot to say about lazy people, and none of it is good! According to Scripture, a lazy person is a "sluggard" who has nothing to look forward to but poverty in his future (*see* Proverbs 6:6-11).

So how do you know if you're being lazy?

A major symptom of laziness is inaction. Lazy people typically waste a lot of time doing nothing productive. Instead of acting on God's Word and obeying the Holy Spirit, they basically choose to do *what* they feel like doing *when* they feel like doing it.

Simply put, laziness is a subtle form of rebellion.

You can often recognize lazy people by their idle, sluggish, and lethargic demeanor. They may sleep long hours and take naps whenever possible. Instead of pursuing their dreams, they're prone to simply sit and vegetate, complaining all the while about how hard and difficult life is for them.

This state of laziness has a tranquilizing effect on your body and mind. If you don't deal with it by getting up and doing something purposeful toward your goals, that lazy mindset will eventually drag you into a state of complete deception. You'll begin procrastinating with your immediate responsibilities, and ultimately you'll waste your life by spending all of your time acting selfishly and foolishly.

Read what the Bible says about sluggards:

How long wilt thou sleep, O sluggard? When wilt thou arise out of thy sleep? Yet a little sleep, a little slumber, a little folding of the hands to sleep: So shall thy poverty come as one that travelleth, and thy want as an armed man.

Proverbs 6:9-11

The sluggard will not plow by reason of the cold; therefore shall he beg in harvest, and have nothing.

Proverbs 20:4

These verses describe sluggards as people who basically lounge around and do nothing. Rather than work and prepare for their future, they simply sit and sleep. Although they may have dreams, desires, and ambitions, they're just too lazy to expend any energy to pursue them.

The Word of God plainly declares that people who fit this description have no future. By refusing to invest time, energy, or hard work into cultivating their gifts and calling, sluggards miss out on all the blessings when the harvest begins to roll in for other people. And if they never choose to change, they will ultimately lose out on ever achieving anything of value in their lives.

Lazy people often complain about having no energy. Of course they have no energy! If a person sits and does nothing for weeks or months on end — watching television programs and sleeping the time away — that person will lose his motivation and have a difficult time getting back into the flow of pursuing important goals. His lethargic behavior will put his body into a state of sedation. And to get his life back on track, that person will have to make the decision to get up and move, regardless of whether or not he feels like it!

Laziness is a choice.

Think about it — how many lazy people do you know who are also successful? I can predict your answer to that question: *None!*

In Proverbs 6:6, the Bible instructs the lazy person to look to the ant. Why does this verse specifically mention the ant? Because the ant is constantly working, building, digging, tunneling, and preparing — without ever taking a minute's break!

There is no creature on earth more industrious and self-motivated than the ant. Just watch an ant hole or ant farm for a while. It's remarkable to see those ants moving so fast, diligently, and consistently — as if the future of the entire world depended on them and their actions.

The book of Proverbs teaches us that this is the way we should order our lives. Yes, we should take a vacation now and then — and, yes, we shouldn't overwork our bodies and push ourselves beyond what is healthy. But, honestly, most of us probably shouldn't worry about overextending ourselves in these areas — because it's likely that we haven't even come close to doing too much work yet!

Our bodies are capable of much more than we think! We barely use one-tenth of our minds' capacity, and many of us eat and sleep far more than is necessary. If we'd study the lives of the people who have really made an impact in this world, we'd find that they worked hard, they pushed themselves, and they were constantly trying to develop their minds to become more creative in the way they accomplished the task at hand.

You can do so much more than your flesh will ever tell you! Your flesh will always say, *Slow down. Don't do any more work. You've already done too much. Give yourself a break! You deserve to sit down for a while and do nothing.* However, you must choose to not listen to these lies of your flesh.

If you've been working really hard all day and you're tired, you should certainly sit down and rest. But don't let your flesh deceive you by telling you that you've already done more than any "average" person would do and you therefore deserve to quit. You were never called by God to be "average"!

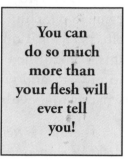

You can do so much more than your flesh will ever tell you!

Maybe you need to turn off the television and get up to clean the kitchen or mow the yard. Or perhaps you should pull out your calculator and checkbook and start correcting all the financial problems you may have created by ignoring your responsibilities. Whatever your particular situation is, I encourage you to stop listening to your flesh tell you how tired you are and make a decision today to contribute something worthwhile to your life!

Another primary characteristic of lazy people is a tendency to overeat. Many lazy people constantly eat because food has become their primary source of companionship and entertainment. If you fall into this category, don't get angry with me. You know it's true!

If you're lazy and overweight, you don't eat just because you're hungry — you eat because you're bored or feeling bad! And to make matters worse, you probably eat the kinds of foods that make you feel more tired. It's a fact that unhealthy foods like potato chips, cookies, fried foods, sugar products, soft drinks, and excessive amounts of meat and fat will actually weigh you down and put you to sleep!

Years ago, I suffered a terrible bout of depression. I prayed and tried everything I knew to change this horrible dread that was consuming my life. I had everything to live for, yet I was so depressed that I didn't want to go on living.

I'll never forget how grateful I was when a visiting speaker came to our church and mentioned in passing the depression-like effects of sugar on people who consume too many sweets. When this man finished speaking, I felt like I had been set free! I turned to my wife and said, "Sweetheart, I think it's sugar! I think that's what's wrong with me!"

That day I went home and cut nearly all the sugar out of my diet. Within one week the awful, dreadful depression that had gripped me for so long was completely gone!

It may not sound deeply spiritual to talk about what we eat, but the fact is that if many of us would change what we eat, we would have more energy. In many cases, the cause of depression is diet-related. If *you've* been battling depression, I encourage you to make healthy changes to your diet and see how much that impacts your overall outlook on life!

Even if you're not dealing with depression or laziness, you still need to watch what you eat. It's simply a waste of your life to spend hour upon hour eating. If you're lonely, get involved in some area of ministry at your church and make some friends. If you need to be entertained, do something productive with your time such as reading a book, devoting more time to developing your business, or finding ways to help other people. Your life is too precious to be thrown away, day after day, doing nothing profitable to your divine purpose.

> **Your life is too precious to be thrown away, day after day, doing nothing profitable to your divine purpose.**

Furthermore, your mind is too sacred to let the world of television fill it with trash and unbelief. Watching too much television often goes hand in hand with overeating. What do you accomplish by watching television hour after hour anyway? Be honest with yourself. All that does is waste a great deal of your precious time while pouring worldly thoughts, pictures, and philosophies into your soul. And afterward, it requires a deliberate commitment of time and effort to deprogram all the garbage you've allowed ungodly, carnal people to feed into your mind.

Instead of filling your mind with worthless television programs, you can choose to get into the Word of God and become renewed in the spirit of your mind (*see* Ephesians 4:23). You can make the decision to "...put off the old man with his deeds; and...put on the new man, which is renewed in knowledge after the image of him that created him..." (Colossians 3:9,10).

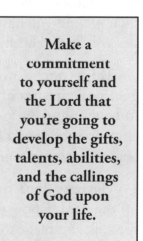

Make a commitment to yourself and the Lord that you're going to develop the gifts, talents, abilities, and the callings of God upon your life.

So make a commitment to yourself and the Lord that you're going to develop the gifts, talents, abilities, and the callings of God upon your life. Defeat laziness, bad eating habits, and television addiction by getting your mind so renewed with the Word that when God calls you to begin a new assignment, you won't even think twice about it!

REASON NUMBER TWO:
UNREALISTIC FANTASIES

If a person is lazy and spends most of his time watching television and eating poorly, he's probably prone to believing unrealistic fantasies as well. Because he isn't following God's plan for his life — enjoying real-life experiences and relationships and living a healthy life — his perception of reality becomes distorted, and his imagination begins to run wild in all the wrong directions.

Rather than working hard to see his dreams manifest, this person sits back and fantasizes about impractical accomplishments and experiences that will never actually become a reality. He hopes for a golden moment in life when he'll magically catch a break without ever having to move a muscle to do his part. He mistakenly assumes that God will simply drop his dream right into his lap one day.

Proverbs 28:19 (*NIV*) has some choice words about people who choose to live in a fantasy world. It says, "Those who work their ground will have abundant food, but those who chase fantasies will have their fill of poverty."

This is one of my favorite verses, and it has been one of the guiding scriptures of my life. According to this verse, if we want to have abundant food — in other words, if we want to experience prosperity and blessing in our lives — we must get up and begin plowing our ground!

Harvests don't happen accidentally! First, you have to break up the hard, fallow ground you're standing on, turn and prepare the soil, and plant some seeds. Then once the soil is prepared and the seeds are planted, you must diligently water and watch over your seeds in order for them to grow and be healthy.

This means regularly walking through your garden to search for the smallest hint of insects, pests, and weeds. You have to get down on your hands and knees to pull out the weeds one by one. Then after many days of careful watching and hard work, your precious seeds will begin to grow and pierce the topsoil, reaching upward to the sun.

Finally, when the plants reach maturity and it's time for harvest, you have to go into the field to reap your crops while they're still ripe and ready. If you let the crops sit too long, bugs will eat them or they'll mildew and rot. Timing is everything when it comes to harvest!

The same is true with your life. Think of your life as a huge garden. If you're going to reap a blessing in your life, it will be because you got involved with the Holy Spirit in making it happen. God will miraculously cause the various areas of your life to increase and grow, but you must do your part by weeding and working the ground in whatever way He directs.

The most important thing you can do when you receive a word from God is work your ground. This may not sound like the most spiritual advice, but it's absolutely true nonetheless. *Working your ground is the only way to see fruit produced in your life.*

In John 15:8, Jesus said, "Herein is my Father glorified, that ye bear much fruit; so shall ye be my disciples." It isn't fun to buckle down and work your ground. You don't see immediate rewards every time you go out to plant a seed in a field. But if you're not willing to work the soil, plant the seeds, pull the weeds, water the growing plants, and wait patiently for your harvest, your fruit will never come. In order for your life to bear fruit, it simply requires a lot of hard work and effort.

You must have a vision of God's plan for your life, and then you must pursue it with all of your spirit, mind, and body. *That's what it means to have a realistic outlook on life.*

Remember, the Bible says you reap what you sow (*see* Galatians 6:7). If you only fantasize about your future and never actually put your hand to the plow, you'll only reap more fantasy, and your future will be utterly devoid of God's blessings. But if you put all of your strength and energy into seeing your dreams become reality, you will successfully move into the next God-ordained phase of your life. With the power of the Holy Spirit working inside and alongside you, you're a guaranteed winner!

Furthermore, it's important to recognize that there is a significant difference between a dream and a fantasy. Dreams are born by the Spirit of God and cause you to strive to be all you can possibly be in Jesus Christ. A true word from the Lord will motivate you and give you the strength to crucify your flesh, say *no* to fear, and strive to continually be conformed to His image.

However, fantasies don't do any of that! They are only temporary, fleeting pauses from reality. Instead of inspiring you to pursue your calling, they lull your mind into a sense of complacency, thus hindering you from doing anything valuable and practical in life. They may temporarily make you feel euphoric, but when the effect wears off and you wake up to reality, you'll see that your kitchen is still dirty, your bills are still unpaid, your marriage is still imperfect, your kids still require correction at times, and your yard still needs to be mowed.

People who passively wait for success to come along may as well kiss their dreams goodbye. The joy and fulfillment they fantasize about will actually go to those who are practical enough to start working their own ground to ultimately reap a harvest of success. These people expect victory to come to them without any effort on their own part. But they just don't understand how life works. Victory, joy, and fulfillment don't float around on a cloud that suddenly and unexpectedly rains down success on their lives. Success is obtained through passion, determination, and hard work — which is why it tastes so sweet when it finally comes!

Fantasizing is easy because it only involves your imagination. But in order to truly find fulfillment, you must hear from God, commit yourself to the dream He gives you to fulfill, and then *go for it* with all your heart. Only a determined pursuit of God's plan for your life will keep you rooted in reality!

Furthermore, a specific word of direction from God will demand that you grow up, change, and allow the Holy Spirit to work in your heart and mind, whereas a fantasy may give you the illusion that success is possible without any effort. Thus, by working your ground instead of living in a fantasy, you'll gain more than a harvest. You'll be changed into the person God has created you to be!

> In order to truly find fulfillment, you must hear from God, commit yourself to the dream He gives you to fulfill, and then *go for it* with all your heart.

REASON NUMBER THREE: SLOTHFULNESS

Another deceptive, subtle, and totally destructive enemy of the believer is *slothfulness*. (You can read more about this subject in Chapter Three of my book, *Dream Thieves*.) Although slothfulness is closely related to laziness, it differs in that it's an *attitude* problem whereas laziness is a *discipline* problem.

> A slothful person chooses to do God's will outwardly, but inwardly he remains neutral and lukewarm toward the things of God.

A lazy person rebels against God's will for his or her life by choosing to do nothing. A slothful person, on the other hand, chooses to do God's will outwardly, but inwardly he remains neutral and lukewarm toward the things of God. He may go through the motions of serving God, saying and doing all the right things, but his fire and passion for serving God has nearly been extinguished.

Concerning slothfulness, the Bible has this to say:

- "The way of the slothful man is as an hedge of thorns..." (Proverbs 15:19).

- "Slothfulness casteth into a deep sleep; and an idle soul shall suffer hunger" (Proverbs 19:15).

These scriptures make it abundantly clear that slothful people, like lazy people, have no future. Their lack of drive and passion to please God causes their lives to become overgrown with weeds — bad habits, neglected strongholds, etc. — that they should have pulled out from the roots long ago. But because they're slothful, they shut their eyes to the problems in their lives and let them continue unchecked. Eventually those problems become so deeply rooted that their lives look more like a confused "hedge of thorns" than a clear path leading to a desired goal!

The Bible also says, "He also that is slothful in his work is brother to him that is a great waster" (Proverbs 18:9). How would you like for your work to be known as nothing but a waste?

This is a good opportunity to ask yourself:

- *What do other people say about me and my work?*

- *Am I known by my peers as an industrious, enthusiastic worker, or do people think of me as a silent partner or a fifth wheel?*

- *What does God think of my attitude?*

- *If I had to stand in front of the Judgment Seat of Christ today, would I be satisfied with the manner in which I carried out God's plan for my life? Or would I be embarrassed, knowing I only half-heartedly and begrudgingly did what God asked me to do?*

The apostle Paul was very aware that he would give account for what he had done with his life. In Second Corinthians 5:9 and 10, he wrote, "Wherefore we labour, that, whether present or absent, we may be accepted of him. For we must all appear before the judgment seat of Christ; that everyone may receive the things done in his body, according to that he hath done, whether it be good or bad."

The day we will all stand before the Judgment Seat of Christ is rarely taught in Christian circles today. This is unfortunate, because our attitude would dramatically change if we were constantly aware that one day we will all stand face to face before the Lord Jesus Christ and give account for how we lived and what our attitude was toward Him and His calling on our lives. There will be no fast talking or excuses on that day!

Slothful people are constantly making excuses for themselves, rationalizing why they didn't keep their promises or why they failed along the way. Instead of honestly admitting that they didn't do what was required, they attempt to hide their lukewarm, "I-don't-really-care" attitude under a worthless heap of excuses.

In Proverbs 22:13, we see the perspective of a slothful man who makes excuses in order to avoid taking action. It says, "The slothful man sayeth, There is a lion without, I shall be slain in the streets." That statement is the equivalent of saying today, "Sometimes earthquakes occur in our state, so I'm going to stay home today in case an earthquake happens."

Talk about stupidity! If a person merely sits around and talks about "what ifs," he'll never achieve anything in life. Yet that's how absolutely ridiculous and absurd the excuses of a slothful person can be. Rather than take responsibility

> **If a person merely sits around and talks about "what ifs," he'll never achieve anything in life.**

and own up to the fact that deep inside he isn't willing to serve the Lord with all of his mind, heart, and strength, he blames his failures and frustrations on everyone and everything else.

But Jesus spoke strongly against excuse-makers. In fact, making excuses was such a serious offense to Jesus that He matter-of-factly stated that excuse-makers will be eliminated from further participation in the plan of God and replaced with those who are more willing.

In Luke 14:16-24, Jesus used a parable to teach about excuse-makers.

> **...A certain man made a great supper, and bade many: and sent his servant at supper time to say to them that were bidden, Come; for all things are now ready.**
>
> **And they all with one consent began to make excuse. The first said unto him, I have bought a piece of ground, and I must needs go and see it: I pray thee have me excused. And another said, I have bought five yoke of oxen, and I go to prove them: I pray thee have me excused. And another said, I have married a wife, and therefore I cannot come. So that servant came, and shewed his lord these things.**
>
> **Then the master of the house being angry said to his servant, Go out quickly into the streets and lanes of the city, and bring in hither the poor, and the maimed, and the halt, and the blind. And the servant said, Lord, it is done as thou has commanded and yet there is room.**
>
> **And the lord said unto the servant, Go out into the highways and hedges, and compel them to come in, that my house may be filled. For I say unto you, That none of those men which were bidden shall taste of my supper.**

Concerning my own staff, excuses are one thing I absolutely don't tolerate. I tell them, "If you've forgotten to do something you were supposed to do, it's better to just take responsibility and say you forgot instead of making up a ridiculous story that doesn't hold an ounce of water. Be honest and upfront about the situation. Making mistakes is forgivable because it's just a part of being human, but please don't make up an excuse!"

Occasionally, conflicts of schedule or responsibility will arise that keep you from fulfilling a prior obligation. When this happens, you shouldn't invent an elaborate reason explaining why you can't do it. The right thing to do in that kind of situation is simply to go to your supervisor and say, "I have other plans that are important to me. May I be released from this particular responsibility?"

Or if you don't want to do a particular task you've been assigned, just ask your supervisor, "Can someone else take on this assignment instead of me?" It's better to do that than to silently grumble about it and then fail to follow through on your responsibility because you just didn't think it was *that* important.

And what should you do if you did fail to follow through on an assignment that was strategic to a major operation? Rather than lay out a detailed story about why it happened, just apologize and admit your failure.

Straightforward honesty defeats slothfulness. You must be honest with yourself and with God about your inner feelings and attitudes. If you continue to make excuses, you're only deceiving yourself and lying to God. And according to the parable Jesus related in Luke 14:16-24, He finds this kind of behavior repulsive.

If you have failed in this area of your life, don't get depressed and beat

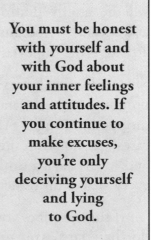

You must be honest with yourself and with God about your inner feelings and attitudes. If you continue to make excuses, you're only deceiving yourself and lying to God.

yourself up — *just do something about it*! Recognize that excuse-making is sin and that you must stop doing it. If you confess your sin in this area of your life according to First John 1:9, God will forgive you and cleanse you of this subtle unrighteous attitude.

Closely related to this sin of making excuses is the sin of blaming other people or outside circumstances for one's own problems. Most of the slothful people I've known in my life blamed their difficulties on the devil, their upbringing, their job, their friends, their family, their pastor, and so on. Because they see every problem as someone else's fault, they never see the need to take responsibility for their own lives.

Even if we've been under some kind of devilish attack, we still have no excuse for failing to obey God. The Bible clearly teaches that Jesus has given us ultimate authority over every demon and Satan himself. (For a detailed study on scriptural spiritual warfare, read my book, *Dressed To Kill*.) A slothful person isn't destroyed by demonic opposition, but by his own lack of passion and diligence to pursue spiritual victory and maturity.

The book of Proverbs plainly teaches that slothful people will be utterly destroyed — personally, spiritually, financially, and socially — because they were too complacent to get up and attend to the important details in their lives.

In addition, Ecclesiastes 10:18 says, "By much slothfulness the building decayeth; and through idleness of the hands the house droppeth through." This verse identifies slothfulness as a "Who cares?" outlook on life. This poisonous attitude leads to laziness and idleness, and slothfulness ultimately neutralizes a person in every area of his or her life.

If this describes you, it's time for you to change! How do you do that? First, you must stop making excuses for yourself and blaming other people for your problems. Next, begin to fellowship with and imitate people who aren't slothful! Hebrews 6:12 says, "That ye be not slothful, but followers of them who through faith and patience inherit the promises." Look to mature believers in your church who have consistently sustained their drive, enthusiasm, and love for the things of God over the years, and then imitate their faith and patience. Spend time with them and become their disciple.

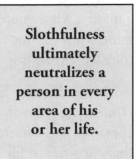

Slothfulness ultimately neutralizes a person in every area of his or her life.

If you can't find anyone who fits this description and can help you reignite the fire in your heart for the things of God, then follow and imitate *Jesus*! Romans 13:14 says, "But put ye on the Lord Jesus Christ, and make not provision for the flesh, to fulfil the lusts thereof."

It's *your* responsibility to renew your mind with God's Word and to pray in the Spirit every day. Doing this regularly as a part of your daily life will not only provide you with the guidance and wisdom you need for each day, but it will also keep your relationship with Jesus thriving and vibrant. Establishing this practice in your life will keep you from ever becoming slothful in your spiritual walk.

REASON NUMBER FOUR:
CREATURE COMFORTS

Creature comforts are the amenities in life that make our lifestyles easy and comfortable. Too often we think that we can't live without them, but, in reality, they are superficial and unnecessary extras. All they do is make life easier and more convenient. Various examples would be microwave ovens, fast-food restaurants, shopping malls, garbage disposals, and dishwashers.

When my family and I first moved to the former USSR during the turbulent and difficult days after its collapse, there were serious deficits of every creature comfort you can imagine. Through our experience of living without those comforts, we gained a whole new perspective on their necessity! Once we had gone without those creature comforts for a while, we realized that they weren't so important after all.

When I return to the States for a visit, it's interesting to me to talk to young people who have grown up with modern creature comforts and therefore tend to consider them as necessities rather than luxuries in life.

During the early years of our lives in the former USSR when we were visiting the United States, one young girl actually asked me, "How do you wash the dishes without a dishwasher?"

"Simple!" I replied. "You fill the sink with hot water and dish-washing detergent, and then you wash the dishes by hand." This girl was horrified by my response. To think that we would have to take an extra ten minutes out of our lives to do something so basic and "old-fashioned"!

Living in the former Soviet Union during those turbulent years taught our family what is and isn't important in life. Water is important; energy to keep our home warm in the winter is important; and food is important. These are the absolute bare necessities of life. However, the modern conveniences that people have come to rely heavily on in their daily lives are *not* fundamental necessities.

I'm talking about extraneous comforts, such as:

- A big house with a beautiful carpet

- A two-car garage with two cars in it

- A new fishing boat parked outside the house

- A microwave oven

- A garbage disposal

- A trash compactor

- A double-wide refrigerator

- A jacuzzi bathtub

- A washer and dryer

- A sprinkler system in the yard

- The newest "smartphone"

As nice as it is to own these amenities, none of them are critical to your existence.

Don't get me wrong. There's nothing wrong with owning creature comforts. In fact, I hope that you have all the nice things I mentioned above. It only becomes a problem if the convenience and comfort those amenities provide make you so snug and warm that you won't leave them behind to take a step of faith!

That's exactly what happened to the children of Israel. Once they were out in the desert heading toward the Promised Land, they began to remember their past life as slaves in Egypt. Egypt had been a difficult and often tormenting place for the Israelites. But after months of traveling through a scorching hot desert and seeing nothing but sand and dust, Egypt started looking pretty good!

The Israelites' memory began playing tricks on them, and the bondage they experienced under Pharaoh became completely overshadowed by thoughts of exotic foods and other niceties. The older generation moaned and groaned and begged to go back to

Egypt so many times, in fact, that God eventually barred them from ever entering the Promised Land.

The truth is that we find out just how serious we really are about fulfilling God's call on our lives when we are asked to give up our creature comforts. It's easy for us to say that we would give everything to Jesus before He ever asks us for anything, and it's easy to say we would die for Him when we live in a country that has religious freedom. But when Jesus finally asks us to step out of our comfort zone into a more challenging walk of faith — leaving behind job security, health insurance, and annual pay increases — we learn just how committed we truly are.

Stepping out of our comfort zone to obey God often requires a deep crucifixion of the flesh.

In Second Timothy 2:5, the apostle Paul wrote about the attitude we need to have in order to obey God's will for our lives. He said, "And if a man also strive for masteries, yet is he not crowned, except he strive lawfully."

> **The truth is that we find out just how serious we really are about fulfilling God's call on our lives when we are asked to give up our creature comforts.**

This word "strive" is the Greek word *athlesis*, which always describes *a full-time, professional athlete who is involved in serious athletic competition*. At the time Paul penned this epistle, there were both amateur and professional athletes. If a person was an amateur, he wasn't considered to be a serious contender. But if he was a professional, he was said to be *striving for the mastery*. This latter kind of athlete was determined to master his profession and become the absolute best in his field. There wasn't an amateur bone in him; *he was totally committed to success.*

By using this Greek word *athlesis*, Paul was asking Timothy, "Are you serving the Lord just for fun? Are you an amateur who isn't really committed to going all the way and accepting the next assignment God is giving you? Are you serving the Lord because it's popular, convenient, and enjoyable at the moment? Or are you a professional, willing to pay any price, undergo any kind of preparation and hardship, bear up under any pressure, and endure it all until you come out a winner? Are you truly committed to finishing the race God has set before you?"

We must regularly ask ourselves these questions. It's fun to serve the Lord when it's easy and convenient, but what if God asks us to step out of our life of ease to accept a bigger challenge? *That's the moment of truth when we find out if we're amateurs or professionals!*

If you're sitting on the banks of your life — fully aware that God is calling you to cross the river and enter a new realm of faith and power — don't look back to Egypt and all of its creature comforts. Look across the river to the land of promise where the milk and honey flows! *Keep your eyes on the milk and honey!*

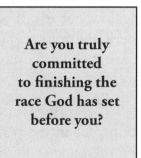

Are you truly committed to finishing the race God has set before you?

Your step of faith will eventually reap incredible fruit — both materially and spiritually. Whatever you give up to follow God's plan for your life will look pale in insignificance once you have found your place in your promised land!

Stepping into the river might bring some discomfort for a period of time. You may have to deal with currents of opposition that you haven't encountered before, and it will definitely require great concentration and wisdom to make it to the other side. But once you've made it past the temporary discomfort and turbulence, you'll reach the banks of the land God has promised you, and the memory of that difficult time will disappear almost instantaneously. One taste of the milk and honey that comes with being obedient to God's good plan, and you'll wonder why it took you so long to get there!

REASON NUMBER FIVE: BELIEVING A BAD REPORT

Let's return once again to our scenario where you are sitting on the banks of the Jordan. God has just given you revelation concerning the next phase of your life, which means you've just realized you'll have to get up and cross that wild, dangerous river. If you focus on the raging, foaming currents before you, you'll become so paralyzed with fear that you'll never be able to move again. Similarly, if you listen to all the doubts and fears that the devil and your friends drop in your ear, every ounce of faith you have will drain out of the bottom of your feet, and you'll never move a muscle!

The world is full of bad reports and doom-and-gloom predictions. Countless people make their livings reporting bad news. Have you ever noticed the kinds of nonfiction books that are bestsellers in today's market? Books flourish when they sport titles like, *The World's Worst Natural Disasters*, *The Tourist Serial Murders*, *The Looming Economic Crisis*, or *The Hidden Dangers of the Airline Industry*. These titles are fictitious, but they make a point. Because of man's sinful nature, people love to hear and watch bad news!

What do you think feeding on all this negative information does to your mind? After reading *The Tourist Serial Murders*, you may never want go on another vacation in your life! And by the time you've read the book on the dangers of airplanes, you'll have lost your peace of mind for your next flight!

Incredible as it seems, people actually buy this trash — and as long as people buy it, others will continue writing it, printing it, and pumping out fear as fast as they can!

What about your local newspaper? If a major newspaper in your city decided to report only good news, how many people would read it? If the evening news reported only good stories, people would be so bored they would turn it off. Disasters sell newspapers. Horror stories make news ratings go up. Bad news is a multi-billion dollar industry!

When our family first moved to the former Soviet Union, international news coverage was completely unavailable since it had been outlawed under the recently deposed Communist government. I'd received a college degree in journalism and had grown to really enjoy watching the news as a part of my daily routine. In fact, before our family moved to the other side of the world, the news had become so important to me that I would sit in front of the television whenever I could, eagerly waiting and watching for the next bit of information to be reported.

Needless to say, when we moved to the former USSR, I didn't know how I was going to live without the news. The way I was thinking about it, you would have thought that the survival of the human race depended on my ability to hear the news!

Adapting to life without any kind of access to international news was a *huge* adjustment for me. Yet somehow I survived those first few years of living overseas when no international news broadcasts were available. In fact, amazingly enough, my life continued to flourish!

In 1992 when the massive riot occurred in Los Angeles and when Hurricane Andrew devastated southern Florida, our family didn't hear about those events until months after they happened. Even then, we only heard about them because an American visitor mentioned them to us in passing. Furthermore, when the political upheaval took place in Moscow during the early 1990s, we wouldn't have even known about it except for the fact that people kept calling from the United States to ask if our family was safe.

Interestingly enough, the only thing that was upsetting our family at the time was all the bad news we were hearing from friends and family in the United States! In the midst of that terrible, potentially revolutionary period in the former USSR, we had absolute peace. We had peace first and foremost because the peace of God was in us and on us to be where we were. But we also had peace because we weren't constantly bombarded with bad news all day long!

Finally, after years of waiting, international English-speaking news arrived in our part of the world. One day while I was opening a bank account at an international bank in Riga, Latvia, I noticed they were broadcasting CNN on the television! When I asked the bank staff how they received it, they told me it was piped into the bank through a special satellite. I was so elated!

Instead of opening a bank account, I decided to pull up a seat and watch a few minutes of the news. However, after only ten minutes, my stomach was literally churning and felt like it was being tied into knots. I told Denise, "Forget this! Life is better without being constantly bombarding by all of this bad news."

In those few minutes of watching news from the United States, I heard about the rise of AIDS. I was informed that the auto and airline industries were on the brink of disaster and that their collapse could cripple the nation financially. I learned of the push to allow homosexuals in the military and of the way the nation's education system was failing. I also learned that the New York Stock Exchange was so high that analysts were afraid it would soon crash.

By the time those few minutes had passed, I felt like my spirit and soul had been violated by informational garbage. At that moment, I truly realized the impact bad reports have on our minds and spirits, and I remembered the Bible's warning to us as believers to continually guard our hearts and minds.

When I was a small boy in Sunday school, we used to sing a song whose lyrics went like this: "O, be careful, little eyes, what you see. O, be careful, little eyes, what you see. There's a Father up above, and He's looking down in love. So be careful, little eyes, what you see."

Then we'd sing the next verse: "O, be careful, little ears, what you hear. O, be careful, little ears, what you hear. There's a Father up above, and He's looking down in love. So be careful, little ears, what you hear."

There's a great truth contained in this little song. We need to be careful concerning what we see and what we hear. Even more importantly, we need to be careful who *interprets* what we see and hear!

For instance, a news story about Israel and the turmoil in the Middle East will be interpreted very differently by a Christian versus a nonbeliever. An unbelieving news commentator who has little or no knowledge of the Bible will simply relate the positive and negative ramifications of a conflict or peace agreement. However, a Bible teacher who understands end-time prophecy will interpret that same report in an entirely different way. The unbelieving news reporter will just report the news and try to make educated guesses about what

> **We need to be careful concerning what we see and what we hear. Even more importantly, we need to be careful who *interprets* what we see and hear!**

could happen, but the Bible teacher will interpret those events according to the Word of God.

In this particular example, it's easy to see how a news story that upsets the peace of countless people can fill you with confidence and joy because you know that Jesus is coming soon! Whoever interprets the news for you is very important. They can either encourage you or hinder your adventure of faith.

Those who influence your thinking have great power over your future.

In Numbers 13, the Bible tells us that Moses sent his delegation of 12 spies into the Promised Land to discover what awaited the Israelites on the other side. The land proved to be incredibly fertile, full of luscious grapevines and large fig and pomegranates trees. In fact, at the brook of Eschol, the spies found clusters of grapes that were so large, they had to be hung from two spears resting atop their shoulders in order to be carried back to the Israelites!

After 40 days of searching out the land, the 12 spies returned to Moses to report what they had seen. They told him, "…We came unto the land whither thou sentest us, and surely it floweth with milk and honey; and this is the fruit of it. Nevertheless the people be strong that dwell in that land, and the cities are walled, and very great: and moreover we saw the children of Anak [giants] there" (Numbers 13:27,28).

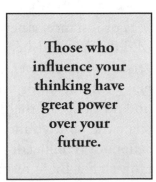

Those who influence your thinking have great power over your future.

Right in the midst of this negativism, one of these spies named Caleb spoke up and silenced the people, saying, "…Let us go up at once, and possess it; for we are well able to overcome it"

(v. 30). Although all of these men were on the same espionage mission, two of the 12 spies — Caleb and Joshua — came back with a radically different interpretation than did the other ten spies regarding what they'd seen and what possibilities awaited them in the Promised Land. The ten spies saw giants, but Caleb and Joshua saw *fruit*.

In fact, when Caleb spoke up to encourage the people to believe they were capable of possessing the land, one of the other spies replied, "...We be not able to go up against this people; for they are stronger than we" (v. 31).

God had miraculously delivered the children of Israel from the bondage of Egypt and brought them to the brink of the Jordan River. Now it was time to step off the banks and take the land they been promised. But instead of trusting God to take care of them, the ten doubting spies were afraid He would forsake them if they took one more leap of faith.

> **The ten spies saw giants, but Caleb and Joshua saw *fruit*.**

Verses 32 and 33 go on to say, "And they brought up an evil report of the land which they had searched unto the children of Israel, saying, The land, through which we have gone to search it, is a land that eateth up the inhabitants thereof; and all the people that we saw in it are men of great stature. And there we saw the giants, the sons of Anak, which come of the giants: and we were in our own sight as grasshoppers, and so we were in their sight."

The report of the ten unbelieving spies was evil because it promoted unbelief in the ability of God.

When your faith is negated, it's impossible for you to move ahead with your life. Your future plans and your dreams are finished the moment you choose to believe that they can't be accomplished. That's why God calls this kind of report *evil*.

Any report that says you and God aren't big enough to do what He has called you to do is evil. If you believe that kind of report, your unbelief will annihilate your future hopes and dreams.

Over the course of many years and through many tests, God showed the children of Israel His unfailing love and patience and brought them to the edge of their destiny. But because they believed the negative report of the ten spies instead of the positive report of Joshua and Caleb, *they were denied their future.*

When the people of Israel heard the report of the ten spies, the Bible records that they wept and moaned through the entire night, crying out, "...Would God that we had died in the land of Egypt! or would God we had died in this wilderness!" (Numbers 14:2).

Moses and Aaron, however, realized the seriousness of the Israelites' unbelief and fell on their faces before God to intercede on behalf of His people. Joshua and Caleb tried to encourage the people as well, declaring, "...The land, which we passed through to search it, is an exceeding good land. If the Lord delight in us, then he will bring us into this land, and give it us; a land which floweth with milk and honey. Only rebel not ye against the Lord, neither fear ye the people of the land; for they are bread for us: their defence is departed from them, and the Lord is with us: fear them not" (Numbers 14:7-9).

> **Any report that says you and God aren't big enough to do what He has called you to do is evil.**

The Israelites were so angry with Joshua and Caleb for their positive, faith-filled report that they threatened to stone the two men to death. But before they could follow through with their threats, the Lord intervened. Filling the tabernacle of the congregation with His presence, God spoke to Moses: "...How long will this people provoke me? and how long will it be ere they believe me, for all the signs which I have shewed among them.... Because all those men which have seen my glory, and my miracles, which I did in Egypt and in the wilderness, and have tempted me now these ten times, and have not hearkened to my voice; Surely they shall not see the land which I sware unto their fathers..." (Numbers 14:11,22,23).

The people of Israel prayed to die in the wilderness, and that is exactly what they received! Because of their unbelief, the Israelites were barred from ever entering the Promised Land and spent the remainder of their lives wandering in the desert. Instead of believing the worst, they should have made a wiser choice when they heard the two reports from the spies.

Had this older generation listened to Joshua and Caleb, they would have entered into the wonderful place that God had prepared for them. As it was, only their children — led by Joshua and Caleb 40 years later — were allowed to enter into the Promised Land and experience victory after victory against the local inhabitants.

In Numbers 14:24, God told Moses why Caleb (and Joshua) would encompass the new leadership of Israel: "...Because he had another spirit with him, and hath followed me fully, him will I bring into the land whereinto he went; and his seed shall possess it."

Joshua and Caleb were men of a different spirit than those of their peers. As I said earlier, these two men saw *fruit* when the other spies saw only *giants*. There was something internally different about Joshua and Caleb that made them focus on *victory* rather than on *bloodshed*, on *accomplishment* rather than on *challenge*.

Twelve men spied out the land together, but each interpreted what he saw based entirely on his own inner attitude. Those who were filled with faith proclaimed, *"We can do it!"* But those who were filled with doubt and unbelief declared, *"We'll die if we try!"* In the end, both groups received exactly what they confessed.

Joshua and Caleb ultimately possessed the land God had promised them, and the other ten spies died in the wilderness, just as they had predicted!

> There was something internally different about Joshua and Caleb that made them focus on *victory* rather than on *bloodshed*, on *accomplishment* rather than on *challenge*.

So be very careful of what you see, what you hear, and, most importantly, who interprets the news to you. Make certain the Word of God is your foundation. Had you been there when the 12 spies returned from the Promised Land to share their reports, whose report would *you* have believed?

We need to be informed of what is happening in the world so we can pray more intelligently, and we need to know what's going on politically so we can voice our opinions and make our will known. That's part of our responsibility as a free people. But we *don't* need to sit around and watch the same disaster reports on the news over and over again. Nor do we need to listen to doom-and-gloom predictions of the future until we become paralyzed from moving forward into the destiny God has prepared for us!

For instance, if God has told you to start a new business, it doesn't matter if the news reports say that the nation's economy is bad for startup businesses. You need to ignore what the news broadcasts are trumpeting and *obey God*! He knew what the news was going to be long before He ever called you to start that business, and He has already devised ways in which you can overcome any obstacle that comes your way.

In closing, I want to mention one possible source of an evil report that can be very sensitive to you — your friends and family.

Your friends and family love you. They don't want you to make a wrong decision in your ministry or career that will harm you or set you back. Thank God that they love you so much!

You need to listen to your family, pay attention to what they say, and then weigh their words according to the Word of God and the leading of the Holy Spirit in your heart. In the midst of their concerns, they may have some godly wisdom you need to heed.

Take all the good counsel you can receive, but draw the line when that counsel produces fear and unbelief. Respect and honor your friends and family members; thank them for their love, concern, and suggestions. However, you must always keep this in mind: It will be you — not your friends or family — who must answer to God for what you do with your life.

Your friends and family want to spare you any hardship as you proceed forward in life. But in order for you to do the will of God, you'll eventually have to face some hardship along the way. If you're establishing a new business, you'll probably have to drastically change your lifestyle in order to succeed. If you're getting married, you will have to learn how to be more sacrificial and accommodate someone else besides yourself.

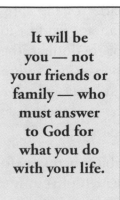

It will be you — not your friends or family — who must answer to God for what you do with your life.

It's good that our friends and family want to spare us difficulty in life, but let's be realistic. We can look at the lives of any of the great men and women of God throughout history and see that they all had to make great sacrifices and work hard to achieve success in their lives.

If you're filled with determination, purpose, and *Holy Ghost guts* — forging ahead against all odds — you can do anything God asks you to do. However, that doesn't mean you won't experience some very difficult and trying times along the way.

Taking the Promised Land was no easy trick! It was true that there were giants in the land (*see* Numbers 13:32). But Joshua knew that the Lord was with the people of Israel and that the giants would therefore be defeated.

Thank your precious family and friends for their love and concern. Listen to their counsel in a way that honors them because they may have some important input that will help you *count the cost*. But, ultimately, you're going to have to do whatever God is requiring of you.

Joshua and Caleb knew exactly what they were up against when they said they were well able to take the land. Having thoroughly explored the Promised Land for 40 days, they had witnessed both the potential blessings and the very real dangers. They'd seen both the great clusters of grapes and the great walled cities of the sons of Anak. These two men weren't living in a fantasy world, nor were they blind or ignorant to the realities of the future. They both had 40 days to ponder and pray about possessing the Promised Land before they stood in front of Israel and declared, *"We can do it."* There was nothing hasty about their faith or their decision.

Hasty decisions usually precipitate hasty failure. Jesus warned us about acting before thinking! In Luke 14:28-30, He said, "For which of you, intending to build a tower, sitteth not down first, and counteth the cost, whether he have sufficient to finish it? Lest haply, after he hath laid the foundation, and is not able to finish it, all that behold it begin to mock him, Saying, This man began to build, and was not able to finish."

Many projects are easy to start, but it's quite another thing to finish them! Don't hastily make major decisions about your future and buy the cart before the horse, so to speak. Find the will of God for your life, and then know it inside and out to the bottom of your soul. Count the cost, and make sure you really understand the assignment that you're agreeing to carry out.

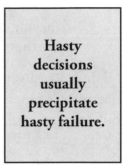

Hasty decisions usually precipitate hasty failure.

That's just common sense!

STEP FORWARD AND
WATCH THE WATERS PART!

After 40 years of wandering in the wilderness, it finally came time for Joshua to step into the waters of the Jordan, cross the river, and go back into the land he had been assigned to spy out years before. He had counted the cost, made his plans, and submitted to Moses for many years in order to prepare for the moment that was upon him.

Joshua had avoided all the pitfalls that could have prevented him from experiencing this point of no return.

- Laziness would have kept him camped on the bank of the Jordan River.

- Unrealistic fantasies would have nullified God's plan for his life.

- Slothfulness would have brought him to ruin.

- The love of creature comforts would have lured him back to Egypt.

- Believing an evil report would have left him dead in the wilderness.

Just like Joshua, you need to make sure that none of these five pitfalls are active in your life. Otherwise, you'll have a very difficult time fulfilling God's plan. Once these hindrances have been crucified by the Word of God and the sanctifying work of the Holy Spirit, the power of God will begin to operate through you in ways you never dreamed possible!

As Proverbs 24:3,4 (*TLB*) tells us, "Any enterprise is built by wise planning, becomes stronger through common sense and profits wonderfully by keeping abreast of the facts." So gather all the facts, being careful about whom you allow to interpret the news for you. Listen to the best advice of your family and friends. Pray and ponder as you fully count the cost.

Then when all is said and done and the Holy Spirit is confirming to your heart that the time is right — *arise and cross the river*. Step forward in faith, and just watch what God does when the soles of your feet touch those raging, whirling, foaming, turbulent waters of impossibility!

Think About It

You may think that questioning your ability is a demonstration of humility, but if God has told you to do something, His command is your enabling power to accomplish that assignment. Therefore, if you have a clear word from the Lord but continue to question your ability to fulfill that task, you doubt God's ability to bring His plan to pass. That is a form of unbelief, which God considers evil because it annihilates faith and brings progress to a screeching halt.

What are some subtle ways that unbelief has gradually diluted your faith and enthusiasm? Have you over-analyzed your situation to the point of doing nothing to move forward in God's plan for your life? Or are you forging ahead tenaciously on your present course while consciously or subconsciously rebelling against God's choice for your next step? Fearful inactivity and self-willed insistence on personal preference are both acts of defiance against God's Word for your life.

❧

We often want to over-spiritualize the keys to success because that makes success seem unattainable in our minds and gives us an excuse to justify failure. Laziness, slothfulness, fantasizing, unwillingness to sacrifice, and distraction are all symptoms of refusing to take responsibility to act. On the other hand, success is based on simple, practical steps that, when acted on, consistently produce the desired consequence. When God has already told us what to do, the first step is to believe Him. The second step is to act on that belief. Believe. Act. Repeat. The ultimate result will be success.

Name three things that you believe you should be doing but have put off implementing in your life. Then answer these questions: What do you think needs to happen before you decide to take action? What are your reasons or excuses for not doing what you know to do? What steps must you take to rectify this situation? Don't fool yourself: Opportunities have an expiration date, and so does your life. Get busy before you run out of time.

CHAPTER SIX

UNDERSTANDING YOUR BOUNDARIES AND PERIMETERS

*I*t's important for us to understand exactly where the Lord wants us to be at any given moment in our lives. If we're in the wrong place doing the wrong thing in any season of our lives, we will only experience frustration, heartache, disappointment, failure, and depression. We'll always be wondering, *Why am I so unhappy and unfulfilled? Why do I always feel like I'm sinking and can hardly keep my head above water?*

Have you ever tried to put a square peg into a round hole? It just doesn't fit! That's exactly what it feels like when you're trying to serve in the wrong place or be someone you were never meant to be! If you are the square peg and either you or someone else you know has been trying to cram you into that round hole, you know precisely the kind of frustration I'm talking about!

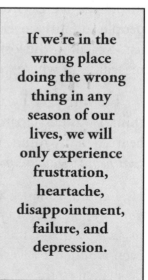

If we're in the wrong place doing the wrong thing in any season of our lives, we will only experience frustration, heartache, disappointment, failure, and depression.

Know Your Calling
and Stick With It

I'm gifted by God to teach the Word of God and to write. I love doing these things! I love to study and prepare messages that I know will enable people to live a more victorious life. And I also love to write, knowing God will use the written page to sharpen believers' understanding and put them on an even surer foundation. That's me! That's what God has called me to do.

For years, I thought I had failed as a Christian because I didn't have an overwhelming desire to be an evangelist who preached to unbelievers. I even tried to force myself to have a burden for sinners, to make myself enjoy preaching evangelistic messages, and to strive to weep for the lost.

Please don't misunderstand me. Through our TV ministry in the former USSR, we have been honored to lead millions of people to Christ over the years, even though I'm not an evangelist. Reaching the lost has always been a priority in our ministry, regardless of where we are or how we are ministering.

But for years, I was hounded by waves of guilt because I didn't think I was passionate enough in my desire to win the lost. I kept hearing in my mind, *What's wrong with you, Renner! Don't you care that people are lost and dying and going to hell?*

I could honestly answer myself, *Yes, I really do care, but I just don't feel the weight of the world on my heart about this. I'm trying to get a burden!* I'd repent for my lack of compassion and at times even wonder if I was really saved. Surely as a Christian, I should be shaken to the core over lost people!

I would pray for strength, energy, and a burning vision to reach a world that desperately needed tracts, booklets, and personal evangelism in order to be saved. I attended special training sessions on evangelism that would last for months. Yet even then, the motivation and drive to be an evangelist never came — which in turn only led to more feelings of guilt. There were times when I felt like I was a total spiritual failure.

However, if someone talked about teaching the Word of God, my heart would immediately respond with joy. And if someone discussed teaching new believers the foundational doctrines of the New Testament, I could hardly keep myself in my seat. The maturity of the saints was such an exciting subject to me that I could hardly contain myself whenever the subject came up! I eventually came to understand the reason I responded this way: God has called me to teach the Bible to believers after they have been won through the evangelistic efforts of others.

Now, of course, this doesn't excuse my personal responsibility to be a witness for Jesus Christ when an opportunity arises. As believers, we each have a responsibility to win the lost, and I haven't neglected this responsibility. Over the years, I have seen countless people come to Christ through my ministry and have personally led many to the Lord. But the primary calling on my life isn't to be an evangelist. I can do the work of an evangelist, as Paul instructed Timothy to do (*see* 2 Timothy 4:5). But first and foremost, I've been called to teach God's Word and to build the Church.

We are not all called to have identical burdens, visions, and job assignments. Each of us has a different role in the plan of God, and every last one of us is vital to fulfilling His will on this planet.

The apostle Paul emphasized this truth in his first letter to the Corinthian church:

> **For as the body is one, and hath many members, and all the members of that one body, being many, are one body:**

so also is Christ.... If the foot shall say, Because I am not the hand, I am not of the body; is it therefore not of the body? And if the ear shall say, Because I am not the eye, I am not of the body; is it therefore not of the body? If the whole body were an eye, where were the hearing? If the whole were hearing, where were the smelling? But now hath God set the members every one of them in the body, as it hath pleased him.

1 Corinthians 12:12,15-18

God chose you, convicted you of sin, drew you in by His Spirit, gloriously saved you, anointed you with His gifts and power, and then placed you in the Body of Christ as it pleased Him. If He has called you to be a Bible teacher, but you're trying to be an evangelist, I guarantee you that you'll feel like a square peg who is being pushed into a round hole. Likewise, if God has called you to be an evangelist but you're feeling pressured to teach the Bible, you're going to feel dissatisfied and out of place until you take your *true* place in God's plan for your life.

> Each of us has a different role in the plan of God, and every last one of us is vital to fulfilling His will on this planet.

Perhaps you're called to an assistant position, a role that you fulfill excellently and with great ease. If others have compelled you to move into an executive leadership role and you're miserable in that position, don't feel like a failure. Just return to doing what you were called and gifted to do!

Many times when people are put into the positions they were never destined to fill, they end up feeling guilty for not liking their job or appreciating their new privileges. Some believers rebuke the devil, thinking he is attacking them in their new prosperity — yet still that nagging sense of uneasiness, guilt, and frustration persists. Others pray for more desire and energy to do the job but never experience it.

If you have accepted an assignment that God never intended for you to accept, here's what you need to understand: Neither rebuking the devil nor praying for more energy is going to help. If you're in the wrong place, you don't have a devil problem or a flesh problem. You're just a square peg trying to fit into a round hole. It's as simple as that!

Blessing and contentment will come when you get back into the place where God wants you to be. Once you're obeying your specific calling, everything will come back into line and your joy will be restored. Your fuzzy perspective will begin to clear up, and you'll know you are back on track again.

The challenge lies in being able to discern your particular situation. You must ask yourself, *Is my flesh recoiling because God is trying to call me upward into new, previously unknown territory, or am I trying to be and do something that He never ordained for me?* Ultimately, only you can answer this question.

Talking with your spouse, your friends, your parents, your pastor, or your employer can help you discern this answer. They may see your situation with more clarity and be able to help you work through the deceptive nature of your own emotions so you can understand what you're really facing. But as I said before, *you're* the one who will stand before Jesus Christ and answer for the gifts, calling, and talents He has placed in your life.

If you're called to stay home as a wife and mother, don't overload yourself by accepting a job with a major corporation. If you're called to work in an administrative role at a large firm, don't try to launch a professional golfing career. If you're called into full-time ministry, don't go out and start a business.

You need to find out exactly where God wants you to be and then to seek His wisdom on how to get there. If you're already following His plan for your life, don't let fantasies of other wonderful careers knock you out of the position in which God has placed you. It may be enjoyable to imagine being somewhere else, far away from all the struggles and realities of your present circumstances. But if that "somewhere else" isn't the place where God has called you to be, in the end it would bring you only hardship and discontentment.

Dreaming of an unrealistic fantasy world will only delay the inevitable fact you must face: God's will for you is the only place you'll find fulfillment and success. Yes, you'll face challenges and difficulties as you pursue His plan for your life. But even if you *could* escape to a deserted island or a remote place in the mountains, you'd find problems there too! Trouble would visit you sooner or later.

In reality, wherever you go and whatever you do, you're going to face problems, challenges, and attacks of the enemy — even when you're in the perfect will of God. But it's a whole lot easier to walk through the fire and flood when you know that you're obeying God and that He has promised to help you every step of the way toward the destiny He's ordained for you!

FACING THE REALITY
OF TAKING THE LAND

As long as you're in this world and want to make a difference, you'll have to face life and deal with it straight on. Trying to ignore or hide from your problems, hoping that they will somehow disappear on their own, is a fantasy of the wildest proportions.

Don't misunderstand me — there is incredible peace, contentment, and joy when we are in God's will. But one of the primary purposes of God's peace in our lives is to undergird us and carry us to victory through the challenges and hardships we face as we serve Him.

The children of Israel dreamed of a beautiful land that flowed with milk and honey, and that land was a real, tangible place. But in order to conquer and possess the Promised Land, they experienced many wild faith adventures in which they faced and overcame great obstacles — including crossing the Jordan River at flood stage (*see* Joshua 3:11-17), taking the city of Jericho (*see* Joshua 6:1-27), battling the inhabitants of Ai (*see* Joshua 7 and 8), defending their treaty with the Gibeonites by fighting five Amorite kings at one time (*see* Joshua 9 and 10), and many more.

The Israelites' confidence in entering the Promised Land was not based on their military might; it was rooted in their rock-solid conviction that they were acting on God's orders. The children of Israel had received a specific vision from God. With that divine word of direction burning in their hearts, they passed over into a land that was full of both conflict and blessing. There they began to experience the reality of what it meant to possess the land!

Regardless of the opposition and difficulties the Israelites faced, they knew they were in the right place at the right time. The challenges they encountered were the normal obstacles that accompany the conquest of any new territory. Enemies had to be eliminated, fear destroyed, rebellion put down, strongholds taken, and many miracles wrought.

Knowing the will of God for your life is vitally important as you undertake any endeavor. It's critical that you understand the boundaries and perimeters of your gifts, callings, and talents. Being aware of your limitations is just as important as knowing your potential. As long as you stay within your boundaries, exactly in the place where God has ordained you to be, it doesn't matter how big the devil looks or how great the obstacles appear to be. You have a promise of divine protection and provision!

In that God-called place, you'll have supernatural joy, peace, and contentment even in the face of giants, because you'll know He has equipped you for victory!

When God called Joshua to lead the people of Israel into the Promised Land, He didn't say, *"Take your pick! Choose any piece of land you want. YOU decide how much land you should have!"* Rather, He gave Joshua a very clear vision of the land that the Israelites were to possess, as well as very specific instructions on how to lead them into it.

God declared to Joshua that every place they set their feet on would be theirs — but He went on to specify where their feet were to go. God said to Joshua, "From the wilderness and this Lebanon even unto the great river, the river Euphrates, all the land of the Hittites, and unto the great sea toward the going down of the sun, shall be your coast" (Joshua 1:4).

Those are pretty clear instructions! God essentially told Joshua, *I'll give you all the land from here to there and from this point to that point.* As long as the people of Israel stayed within those perimeters, they would be directly in the middle of God's divine plan — and could therefore be assured of His divine assistance as they proceeded forward.

God didn't promise to give the Israelites Egypt, Assyria, or any of the lands to the far north. He made it very clear exactly which lands they were to possess. If they moved beyond those particular boundaries, their success was *not* guaranteed.

As long as God's people stayed in the place where He had called them to be, they could be absolutely confident of receiving His supernatural help.

Biting Off More Than You Can Chew

One of the most embarrassing things to me is when ministers or Christian businesspeople publicly announce that they are going to move forward on a project that sounds wonderful and exciting — but then they run out of money and can't finish the job. This brings a reproach on the ministry or Christian business and on the Church at large.

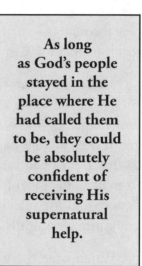

As long as God's people stayed in the place where He had called them to be, they could be absolutely confident of receiving His supernatural help.

In most situations when this happens, the root of the problem can be found in one conclusion: Despite these leaders' good intentions, they have wandered out of their primary calling to do something God never called them to do in order to meet a need He never called them to meet. There are exceptions to this, of course; however, this is usually the case.

How many Christian schools have been started that God never initiated? How many well-meaning believers have launched programs to feed the poor when God only called them to teach His Word? How many people, truly called by God to have a radio or television ministry, proceeded too hastily with their vision and then later had to make desperate appeals for money because they couldn't pay their radio or television bills?

We've all seen situations like this — and if we're in business or ministry, we've probably made similar mistakes. However, even in our personal lives, we've experienced those times when we've started out with a budget for remodeling our house, moved to a new office, or purchased a few new articles of clothing, only to overstretch ourselves financially in the process. How easy it is to go beyond what we planned to spend! One way or another, we've all bitten off more than we could chew.

This is even easier to do when one has a mandate from God to reach huge masses of people. When a minister sees millions of people who desperately need to hear the Gospel and the teaching of God's Word, it becomes extremely difficult — almost a heartbreaker — for him or her to say no to any opportunity to reach people for Christ.

There have been times when I've had to say to myself, *Someone else will have to do this because I can't be led by every need I see, and I can't afford to do any more at this moment.* Personally, my greatest challenge has been in knowing when *not* to expand our outreaches in the former USSR. For instance, I sometimes have to make a decision between saying, "All right, I'll accept another new region for television in the former USSR," or, "We can't do any more; enough is enough for now."

When I see the great need of the people of the former Soviet Union and all the doors that are open to our ministry, my natural inclination is to walk through every last one of them. However, although the Gospel is free for the lost, it requires a great deal of money for its ministers to preach it! Television and production time, staff salaries, stamps, churches, crusades, and printing literature — all of these require a great investment of money, time, and manpower. Every time I stop to consider the amount of money that has flowed through our organization since 1991 for our TV ministry, I'm left speechless. Sometimes it requires a great deal of money and manpower to fulfill what God tells us to do!

Lack of vision has never been a problem for me. My greatest challenge in ministry has been in knowing how quickly or how gradually to carry out my vision. In order to fulfill the dream God has put in my heart without making major errors that would create a financial crisis, I have to stay on my knees in prayer and constantly strive to be sensitive to the voice of the Holy Spirit.

In those times of seeking the Lord for direction, I look at our financial records to see whether or not we can immediately handle another big assignment. If I have a green light in my spirit to take on a new project, I'll do it by faith even if I don't know where the money is coming from.

However, most often — and this may come as a shock to you — I've found that the Lord leaves it to me to make the decision based on the natural circumstances and resources I have to work with. As Proverbs 24:3,4 (*TLB*) tells us, "Any enterprise is built by wise planning, becomes strong through common sense, and profits wonderfully by keeping abreast of the facts." Sometimes it seems that the Lord has opened a huge door of opportunity in my life, but I haven't sensed a direct word from the Holy Spirit concerning the matter. In those situations, I have to do some serious thinking, praying, and planning before I make a decision about that particular opportunity.

As believers, we must be people of both faith and common sense. Today this is a rare mixture indeed! Some decisions in life are based on a specific word from the Lord, but many are based more on open doors of opportunities that are presented to us. By exercising common

> **As believers, we must be people of both faith and common sense. Today this is a rare mixture indeed!**

sense and following the direction that brings peace in our hearts as we pray, we determine which doors we should walk through and which ones we should not. That may not sound too spiritual, but that's often how God leads us.

I must tell you that I also lean on the solid counsel of advisors whom God has placed in my life, and I listen very carefully to what other members of my team have to say. God has provided people who are smarter than I in the business realm, as well as key staff members who are more gifted than I in other crucial areas. So I have learned the wisdom of *listening* to what others have to say. As Proverbs 15:22 (*NKJV*) states, "Without counsel, plans go awry, but in the multitude of counselors they are established." Ultimately I know that I must make the final decision regarding how to proceed and that my advisors and team members will support me once a certain direction has been determined. But over and over again, my willingness to listen to others has saved me from disasters and helped us chart a successful path through turbulent territory where we have no one else to follow.

I know it seems like it would be more exciting to be led every time by prophecies and visions that come dramatically in the night. But I don't know anyone in the world who is led only in these more spectacular ways. Even the most well-known prophetic ministers in the Body of Christ don't base all of their decisions on supernatural revelation.

Look at people who have succeeded. They are filled with faith, courage, guts, brains, and common sense. They move ahead by faith — but what do they do when they've pushed their faith to the limit and they know they're pushing too far and too fast? *They stop, seek God for wisdom, and regroup.* Then afterward, when they're feeling more confident, they begin moving ahead again.

What if the vision God gives us is very general, such as the divine assignment Denise and I received in the early 1990s: to teach His Word on television in the former USSR? That was a very large vision for us! We had to discern whether or not God was saying, *"Go after ALL that's available to you right now!"* Hundreds of thousands of dollars would have been needed to pursue that course. But since our financial resources were limited, we decided we were supposed to take a more commonsense approach to fulfilling our vision. We determined to allow the Holy Spirit to lead us — carefully, step by step.

It's important not to move ahead so quickly that you don't have the cash flow to pay for your vision.

Again, this may not sound very spiritual, but the reality of serving God is this: Moving ahead too quickly without the resources to pay for your vision spells one thing: **D-I-S-A-S-T-E-R!**

Keep in mind that when the children of Israel passed over the Jordan River into the Promised Land, they didn't attempt to take the entire land all at once. They possessed the land one piece at a time.

Most likely, that's how each of us will fulfill our vision as well — step by step. I'm just speaking honestly. Most of us probably aren't mature enough to handle the pursuit of our God-given assignment more quickly than that anyway!

TAKING ONE STEP
AT A TIME

In Joshua 1:2, God commanded Joshua, "...Go over this Jordan, thou, and all this people, unto the land which I do give to them, even to the children of Israel."

If the children of Israel were anything like typical people today, they probably danced with joy when they heard this prophetic word that declared they were finally getting ready to cross into the Land of Promise! I can almost hear them exclaiming, "It's here! Our day has come! He's giving us the land!"

However, God went on to tell them, "Every place that the sole of your foot shall tread upon, that have I given unto you..." (Joshua 1:3). God was going to give them their inheritance — but it would be *one step at a time*. What wisdom this displayed on the part of God! Although the land belonged to the Israelites by virtue of His promise, all kinds of catastrophes would have been created if they had tried to immediately possess the entire land. The land was so new to them that they needed time to understand and get familiar with what had been given to them.

God designed His plan so that the children of Israel would conquer each new territory as they walked across it. Consequently, by the time they had fully possessed a region, they would have come to know that land well. They would have smelled it, examined it, searched it out, and fought for their lives on it. Putting their feet on that ground prepared them to manage the land once it was theirs.

If God had dropped His entire plan into the laps of the Israelites without any involvement on their part, they wouldn't have known what to do with it! If they had tried to cope with all the regions of the Promised Land simultaneously, they would have been completely overwhelmed by the diverse multitude of obstacles they encountered each step of the way. What a mess that would have been!

But it *didn't* happen that way because of God's wisdom. He knows that success doesn't just fall out of the sky and land on our front door one morning. Step by step, we must take the territory He has promised us. As we take each additional step, we become more acquainted with the destiny to which God is calling us. We gain experience, and we learn to anticipate what lies ahead.

As we move forward in our new assignment, we begin to see that each step we take prepares us for the steps God desires us to take in the future. Furthermore, by possessing our new territory one step at a time, we're able to deal with each challenge we encounter *separately* — which is much better than having to fight all of our battles at the same time!

You may stumble and fall during your first few steps in faith, but that doesn't mean you've failed. It only means you've momentarily lost your balance, just as a child does when he first attempts to walk. Stumbling and falling is a necessary beginning phase of learning to walk.

> As we move forward in our new assignment, we begin to see that each step we take prepares us for the steps God desires us to take in the future.

If a baby falls after taking his first steps, you don't cry about it. Instead, you just stand him back up and say, "Let's try it again!" Few babies just hop to their feet one day and start walking. First, a baby has to crawl. Then he has to use a piece of furniture to pull himself up to his feet. And then, finally, looking a little uncertain, he lifts his foot to take his first tentative step forward.

After a few falls and bruises, that baby will eventually take three or four steps in a row without falling. Even if he hits the floor after those few steps, his face will still beam with exhilaration over his accomplishment. To that baby, those first steps are as exciting as climbing the world's tallest mountain would be to a seasoned mountaineer!

For a baby to grow up as a healthy child and adult, his development has to begin with those first, tiny steps. If a baby never attempted to crawl or walk, it would be very apparent that something was wrong.

Likewise, your first steps may seem huge and monumental. But the truth is, the only thing really historic about those first steps is that you obeyed God and you *took* them. Without those first steps, you wouldn't have been able to take all the other steps God has designed for your life!

If you've never taken a step of faith since you've been saved, it's a signal that something is very wrong with you spiritually. The Bible plainly teaches that the just shall live by faith (*see* Habakkuk 2:4, Romans 1:17, Galatians 3:11, Hebrews 10:38) — a principle that is of the greatest significance.

You'll never know the thrill of living for God until you have stepped beyond your own abilities into the realm of faith. As one believer put it, "The just shall live by faith — and if he doesn't, he never really learns to live!"

When God tells you, *"I will give you every place that the sole of your foot treads upon,"* He means it. He's saying to you, *"The land is yours — now come and get it! The minute you place your feet on it, you can have it!"*

Isn't it amazing how God requires us to grow and change as we move into each new assignment in our lives? He could have made it easy by just thrusting us forward quickly or by dropping new blessings into our lives without any involvement on our part. But if God did that, it would defeat part of His purpose.

> **God wants to *change* us in the process of blessing us.**

God doesn't want to just bless us. He wants to *change* us in the process of blessing us. If the dreams and desires He's planted in our hearts came to us too easily, no faith would be required; no crucifixion of our flesh would be demanded; and we would never grow and become conformed to the image of Jesus Christ.

God's plan for your life won't be finished until you're fully conformed to His Son. As Romans 8:29 states, "For whom he did foreknow, he also did predestinate to be conformed to the image of his Son...."

As you take each new step of faith, God will reveal flaws in your character that need to be eliminated. In order to fulfill your assignment, you'll have to correct these problematic areas in your life.

However, if you deal with these flaws with the help of the Holy Spirit, you'll reach a new and greater level of maturity, which will enable you to take the next step of faith with even more confidence and ease. Through time and experience, you'll keep growing in wisdom and maturity — and the day will come when you'll *eagerly* accept the next big challenge God brings your way, no matter how impossible it seems!

BE SPECIFIC AND REALISTIC
ABOUT YOUR VISION

God gave the children of Israel a very specific vision of the Promised Land. In Joshua 1:4, He told them, "From the wilderness and this Lebanon even unto the great river, the river Euphrates, all the land of the Hittites, and unto the great sea toward the going down of the sun, shall be your coast."

God knows that His people need clear directions in order to stay on track. He didn't tell the Israelites, *"Take any piece of land you want. Your inheritance is up to your own choosing!"* Instead, His command was very clear, to the point, and nearly impossible to misinterpret. In essence He was telling them, *"From point A to point B is your ground — and no more!"*

God gave the people of Israel direction and enabled them to set their sights on a concrete dream. They had a goal to shoot for as they crossed over into that land.

God knows that human beings need direction and purpose. It's their nature to want discipline, boundaries, borders, and goals for their lives. When people have nothing to look forward to or to work toward, they tend to wander off course and create confusion in their lives by trying to set their own agendas and find their purpose on their own.

Children need boundaries, whether or not they realize it at the time. If a child's parents *don't* set boundaries for him, that child will grow up rebellious and disrespectful toward them and toward God. First Samuel 3:13 teaches us that Eli destroyed his sons because he didn't love them enough to set boundaries in their lives and discipline them.

Proverbs 13:24 also clearly admonishes us to discipline our children and set clear boundaries for them. If we fail to do this, we set them up for a future filled with destruction.

Likewise, when leaders fail to provide their organizations with clear goals and direction, they open the door for failure, discouragement, depression, poverty, and faithlessness to take hold in their people. They may also be leaving the door open for someone in the organization to step forward and say, "If no one else will lead you and give you direction, look to me — I will!"

Most organizational and church splits could have been avoided if the leadership had been more specific and focused on the future. People need something to look *toward*! If a leader doesn't provide a vision, his people will look elsewhere to find new direction and leadership. This principle has been proven time and time again throughout history!

Proverbs 29:18 says, "Where there is no vision, the people perish: but he that keepeth the law, happy is he." People need purpose and a plan for their lives. If they don't have that, they will never become all they were intended to be.

If you're a parent, take the time to give your children something to shoot for. Impart dreams of greatness to them! Help them see themselves becoming godly leaders further on in their lives. Likewise, if you own a business, set goals for your staff and salespeople. Don't expect them to be the visionaries of your company. You are their leader! They need your vision, your faith, and your ideas about the future. Help them see where your company is headed and what the dividends will be for those who are faithful.

If you're a pastor, you need to ask God what His plan is for your congregation and then clearly explain that vision to them. The nation is speckled with thousands of little churches that will never do anything significant because they have no specific direction. Don't let that be your church! God has called you and your people to do more than just come to a building to see one another, sing a few songs, and hear a nice message once a week. You can change the history of your town or city and the entire surrounding region if you will get God's vision for your church firmly planted in your heart and then begin carrying it out with everything in you!

GET *GOD'S* PLAN

Occasionally, I hear young preachers say, "We're going to take the whole world for Jesus!" This is a mistake. You should be realistic with your goals. You aren't going to take the whole world for

Jesus — and even if you did, you wouldn't know what to do once you had finished taking it! You may be called to advance God's Kingdom into a significant part of the world. But you personally — your ministry or your church — are never going to win the entire world for Jesus. It's ridiculous to even make such a statement!

The apostle Peter was specifically called to the Jewish world, and the apostle Paul was specifically called to the Gentile world. It is especially clear in the ministry of Paul that when he tried to move beyond his primary call to the Gentile world and focused instead on his Jewish brethren, he nearly always encountered problems (*see* Acts 13:45-14:6). There are consequences when we move beyond our God-given boundaries. This principle holds true for all of us.

Rather than focus on goals that are far too broad to be realistic, seek God for His specific vision for you. What part of the world does God want you to reach? By what means are you supposed to reach it? God didn't tell Joshua, *"Here is the world, young man! It's all yours!"* Instead, God gave very clear boundaries and limitations to him as He instructed Joshua to lead Israelites into the Promised Land.

> There are consequences when we move beyond our God-given boundaries.

If you live in a city of several million people — or even in a city of several thousand — I seriously doubt that God is going to give you the *entire* city. But He *will* give you a portion of your city! Which part of the city does God wish to give you? The north side? The south side? The east side? The west side? Maybe He wants to give you a specific part of the population — such as the youth, the senior citizens, the homeless, the high school students, the executive community, etc.

Whenever God declares to you, *"THIS is your portion"* — it then becomes *your* responsibility to *step out in faith and possess that promised land.*

PRAY TO RECEIVE
THE DIVINE STRATEGY

Prayer is essential to fulfilling your vision. Not only is it the only way you're going to discover the specific boundaries and perimeters of your vision, but it's the only way you will discover *how*, *when*, *where*, and *with whom* you are to proceed.

You're not going to open your Bible one day and read, "You, [insert your name], shall take [name of your hometown] for God! The Lord will ask you to establish a church on Main Street the first year. Then over the following three years, He will have you add a children's school, housed in the warehouse across the street from the church. The Lord will lead you to hire Brother So-and-so to run the children's school, and two years later, He will tell you to start a Bible school."

To receive that kind of specific direction, you'll have to spend quality time with the Holy Spirit — but even then, He will usually give you the plan one step at a time.

If you're a pastor, you need to determine the next practical step God wants you and your church to take to bring Jesus Christ to the people of your city. How do you put your foot on that ground and claim it for your own? And then how do you move forward to actually *possess* that ground and fulfill that particular assignment?

One thing is certain: Nothing will ever happen if you and your congregation just sit in your church building and pray for the city to become yours. I've seen hundreds of churches who have made the mistake of believing revival would come to them without any effort on their part. On the contrary, if you want to reach your city for Jesus Christ, you have to get out of your church building and touch people's lives with God's love and with the truth of the Gospel *in addition* to praying!

One of the reasons we pray about revival in our churches is not just for God to pour out His Spirit, but also to receive His divine strategy and plan to achieve it.

Charismatic churches tend to do more praying than acting. Although they pray with the greatest of intensity, many lack a strategy to see revival come to pass. As a result, many of these churches fail to live up to their full potential. Their devotion to prayer is wonderful example to follow. *Prayer is the foundation for revival!* Every major revival in history has been preceded by a strong season of prayer in the Church. However, prayer without strategy is insufficient to see a great move of God come to fruition.

> **One of the reasons we pray about revival in our churches is not just for God to pour out His Spirit, but also to receive His divine strategy and plan to achieve it.**

There are exceptions, of course. A few Charismatic churches *do* have a step-by-step plan on how to affect their city and the nation. And because of their preparation and strategy, those churches are usually the fastest-growing churches in the country. Everyone takes note of them and wonders how they're doing it!

On the other hand, many evangelical churches are more aggressive with their outreach to the lost than most Charismatic churches and have therefore established a reputation for growing steadily throughout the years. I've heard Charismatic pastors from across the nation comment on how remarkable it is that some of these evangelical churches are so consistent in their growth patterns.

There is a reason for this consistency. These evangelical churches work as hard as they can to reach their cities for Jesus Christ! They often have established visitation nights, work days, and schedules for calling everyone on their membership roll to remind them of the vision to reach the lost. Their vision is regularly set before their congregations.

I grew up in this type of church and later served in a pastoral capacity in a large evangelical church. So I'm well aware that the prayer emphasis is often lacking in these churches that work so hard at reaching the lost in their cities. Yet without an understanding of authoritative, Spirit-led prayer about a matter, it's very easy to implement a plan that man has deemed effective but that is not *God's* strategic plan for that time and place.

You must walk out both the spiritual and the practical sides of God's plan to achieve victory in any area of life.

Simply praying in general terms isn't enough. You have to ask the Holy Spirit for a specific, detailed strategy and then do exactly what He tells you to do. If you follow a plan that only *seems* right because it's the way your denomination has always done it, you won't be operating from a spiritual foundation. Consequently, God won't be able to support the manmade plan you're trying to achieve.

You must build a foundation to sustain your vision, and only prayer can build that foundation.

> **Simply praying in general terms isn't enough. You have to ask the Holy Spirit for a specific, detailed strategy and then do exactly what He tells you to do.**

Start with a dream that the Lord plants in your heart. Then with *all* your heart, seek God in prayer to understand what He wants you to do with that dream. Once you know what you're supposed to do and how you're supposed to do it, put all of your mind, heart, strength, and energy into your assignment. *Pray like the success of the entire project depends completely on God, but work like the success of the entire project depends completely on you.* This powerful combination of prayer and hard work always produces marvelous fruit in the Kingdom of God.

If you desire to move further ahead in your ministry, company, or profession, how are you going to accomplish that goal? By sitting at your desk and simply thinking about your future? I promise you, that won't accomplish *anything*.

Regardless of your present position in life — whether you're a businessperson, minister, college student, etc. — you have to begin your dream by asking the Holy Spirit to impart a plan, an idea, an objective, and a strategy to get from where you are to where you want to be. Your new assignment won't come to you by itself. You have to take one step at a time, steadily moving toward your goal — until your goal is finally realized and that place of promotion is yours at last!

ALLOW GOD TO EXPAND YOUR BOUNDARIES AND DIMINISH YOUR LIMITATIONS

Consider a lowly janitor who has a wild, outrageous dream of one day becoming the president of the company he works for. I seriously doubt that this aspiring janitor will be promoted directly from the janitorial department to the president's office. It's great that he has a huge, exciting vision. But how is he going to move from the cleaning closet to the executive lounge?

Or what if a student who only makes average grades wants to do better scholastically? How is that student going to achieve that goal?

What if a father and mother want to be better parents? How are they going to improve their skills in parenting?

What if husbands and wives sense that they're failing in their marital roles and that they truly want to save their marriages and become the best spouses they can possibly be? At that moment, these spouses have a huge challenge in front of them. They have to answer this all-important question: *What steps are they both going to take to fix their marriages?*

It's incredibly rare that you can achieve such goals overnight. So how do you make major changes in your life? How are you going to get from point A to point B?

First, you must become more specific in the way you pray. Focus on this one question as you seek God in prayer: *How do I proceed toward the goal that You've planted in my heart, Lord?* When you pray like this, God will begin to give you the ideas and steps you need to move gradually and steadily toward your goal.

God told Joshua and the children of Israel that the Land of Promise would be theirs as they took it *step by step.*

By the way, that's exactly how God will reveal your future to *you* as well — *step by step.* The beauty of this method is that with each step, you will change and grow. And as you move forward, God will broaden your vision. Your vision will grow little by little, giving you more and more confidence that the power of the

> **Focus on this one question as you seek God in prayer: *How do I proceed toward the goal that You've planted in my heart, Lord?***

Holy Spirit is working in your life, helping you accomplish what you once thought was impossible.

Each step may seem tiny at the moment. But if you turned around and looked at where you used to be — a few steps back from where you are right now — you probably wouldn't even recognize your old self! It's amazing how all those tiny steps eventually bring forth such a radical transformation.

On the other hand, if your natural way of thinking seems too small right now, it won't take a very large vision to really begin stretching you. For instance, if you live in a small town and you've never been out of your state, your decision to take a trip to New York City may sound like the greatest adventure imaginable! You may even feel like you've conquered the world (or at least the Big Apple!) because you've done something so brave and daring.

Yet in reality, that one experience will change your perspective of the world. You will have seen life beyond your hometown — a part of life that you never saw before. And if you see other parts of the United States or perhaps other parts of the world, your perspective will continue to be radically changed.

When you finally return to your hometown, you'll realize how small your world was in that earlier period of your life. How unfortunate it would have been if you'd only stayed within your small, comfortable bubble and thus missed out on God's great plan for your life. But, sadly, that is exactly what many people tend to do!

The vision God places in your heart will always amount to something bigger than you, something you *can't* do without the help of the Holy Spirit. All you can do is to prayerfully and diligently start taking small steps, orchestrated by the Lord as He endeavors to lead you toward the wonderful destiny He has ordained for you.

If you walk in those steps, you'll grow, mature, change, and expand in your walk with God. Eventually you'll look back in absolute awe at the way the Holy Spirit brought you from that first tiny step of faith to the giant leaps of faith you can now take with confidence.

Success, joy, and fulfillment begin with knowing God's specific plan for your life and then pursuing that divine plan with diligent, faith-filled prayer. Then you must work within the boundaries and perimeters He has set for you by asking the Holy Spirit for the divine strategy to carry it out. Once you have His plan, you must take one step of faith at a time, growing and expanding throughout the process.

> The vision God places in your heart will always amount to something bigger than you, something you can't do without the help of the Holy Spirit.

As you move ahead in obedience and faith, you'll discover the greatest and most delightful surprise of all: God's Spirit will work alongside you with supernatural wisdom and power beyond your wildest dreams!

You have to begin pursuing your dream by asking the Holy Spirit to impart a plan, an idea, an objective, and a strategy to get from where you are to where you want to be. Your new assignment won't come to you by itself. You have to take one step at a time, steadily moving toward your goal — until your goal is finally realized and that place of promotion is yours at last!

Think About It

Just as you must know your strengths and weaknesses, you need to know the boundaries of what you are to do and be realistic about the God-given gifts and equipment you have to work with. When you focus your efforts on cultivating your strengths and being proficient in your own "place of grace," you will multiply your effectiveness to a seemingly limitless degree.

What is that gift or ability that is unique about you — the quality that seems to affect those around you in such a positive way? That particular characteristic is linked to your destiny. Are you engaged in activities on a daily basis that will develop this quality God has deposited in you? What are some ways you can be a blessing to others through the use of that specific gift or ability? Are you neglecting that gift because it seems small or unspectacular? Or are you possibly trying to do something that interests you — but that you're not equipped to do?

You may need to have an honest conversation with someone who really knows you and has a vested interest in your success. In Christ you can do all things, but He has not called you to do everything. What are your particular boundaries?

❦

Specific prayer enables you to receive wisdom concerning the specific details you need to know. An effective plan is made up of practical steps that point you in the right direction. God will never tell you everything all at once. He expects you to follow Him by faith, one step at a time. But as you seek His guidance through His Word and in prayer, the Holy Spirit will download divine instruction into your spirit concerning what, when, where, how, and with whom you are to take action.

Are you lacking some key points of insight regarding how to fulfill the God-given dream in your heart? You may sense it's time to move forward — but do you know in which direction? What was the last step God told you to take? Have you completed it? If so, take some time in prayer to seek the Lord. Then you will know as you follow on to know the Lord (Hosea 6:3).

CHAPTER SEVEN

BE STRONG AND COURAGEOUS!

Where did Joshua get his strength and courage? The answer is found in Joshua 1:5. Before Joshua marched toward the Jordan River, God made a promise to him, saying, "There shall not any man be able to stand before thee all the days of thy life: as I was with Moses, so I will be with thee: I will not fail thee, nor forsake thee."

That's an incredible promise.

The exciting news is that the promise God made to Joshua applies to us today! If we're in the middle of God's will for our lives — doing what He has asked us to do, regardless of any opposition, situation, or problem — no human being or earthly circumstance is big enough to stop us from fulfilling our assignment.

You might be thinking, *Does God really promise that He'll be with me as He was with Moses?* Well, consider the prayer Jesus prayed for us in John 17 — that we would be one with the Father as *Jesus* is one with Him (*see* John 17:11). Since our spiritual inheritance under the New Covenant includes the measure of God's presence and promises in our lives that Jesus experienced when He walked on this earth, certainly we can claim any promise that God made to Moses and Joshua under the Old Covenant! So according to Joshua 1:3, God will remove *any* obstacle from our path — even if it means parting the Red Sea and the Jordan

River — in order to help us get the job done! With God on our side, we can be certain of victory.

God went on to promise, "...I will not fail thee, nor forsake thee." With the knowledge that all the power of Heaven is on your side, you can begin to throw off every hindrance and start taking the first necessary steps toward fulfilling God's plan for your life.

What about opposition? Everyone experiences it! Even if you always stayed home, watched television, and did nothing all day, you wouldn't eliminate opposition from your life. Instead, you'd just deal with a different form of opposition. If you just sat around all day and ate junk food, you'd eventually grow lazy and overweight. This in turn could potentially make you become unattractive to your spouse and lead to serious marital problems. In addition, because you never did anything exciting, you might become jealous and critical of those who do. And as your children watched your behavior, they'd likely learn from your example, growing up to be unproductive and lacking any incentive to make something of their lives. Then when you wish they *would* grow up and move out of the house, they won't!

> Since you can't escape opposition by deciding to stay passive and do nothing, you may as well choose the kind of opposition you want to face in life.

Since you can't escape opposition by deciding to stay passive and do nothing, you may as well choose the kind of opposition you want to face in life. Do you want problems that result from doing nothing — or do you want to face challenges that result from tackling divine assignments that others call impossible?

I've already made my choice, and today I'm seeing my children dream big and fulfill the will of God for their own lives. It's so amazing and gratifying!

They are making right choices and seeing God's plan come to pass for their lives just as Denise and I have seen His will fulfilled in our own lives.

Take God's words to Joshua and make them your own today: "No man will be able to stand before me all the days of my life. As God was with Moses, so He will be with me. He will not fail me nor forsake me as I follow His will for my life!"

LEADERSHIP CRISIS
IN THE WORLD TODAY

When Joshua stepped into his role as the new leader of Israel, the people were experiencing a leadership crisis. Moses had been dead for 30 days, and the Israelites were wondering, *Who will lead us? Who will show us where to go? Who will speak to God on our behalf?*

In the midst of this instability, the word of the Lord came to Joshua as God called him into the position of leadership for which he had spent many years training. After promising to be with him as He had been with Moses, the Lord went on to command Joshua, "Be strong and of a good courage: for unto this people shalt thou divide for an inheritance the land, which I sware unto their fathers to give them" (Joshua 1:6).

I want you to particularly notice God's opening command to Joshua: *"Be strong and of a good courage...."* One thing the world desperately needs today is leaders who are willing to take a stand and do what is right, regardless of whether or not it's politically correct. Leaders who are strong and courageous are very scarce, both in the world and in the Church.

We live in a time when most leaders go out of their way to be politically correct and avoid offending anyone. Very few are willing to make critical decisions or take a stand that might jeopardize their own future job security. This is precisely what's wrong with politics in western nations like the United States. For the most part, no one is willing to lead because no one wants to offend.

When a person is promoted into a position of leadership, he will often try to walk on eggshells at first because he wants to be liked and doesn't want to offend anyone. In essence, he wants to be the friend of the people. However, there is no way for an effective leader to be a friend of the people! Not everyone is going to like him, appreciate him, or agree with him at all times.

If you try to please everyone, you'll end up pleasing no one, and you certainly won't please God.

What if you make a decision that offends someone? What if you make a statement that isn't politically correct? What if you upset a special-interest group and, as a result, they oppose your reelection? *What if? What if? What if?*

> **If you try to please everyone, you'll end up pleasing no one, and you certainly won't please God.**

Many times politicians are so controlled by their fear of man that their leadership is paralyzed from the moment they take office. They become tossed to and fro by special-interest groups who finance their reelection campaigns, and they go out of their way to not appear bigoted or close-minded. In fact, politicians often owe so many favors to people that they are controlled by special-interest groups even before they are elected. Eventually they forget why they were sent to public office in the first place — *to represent the people.*

Those who fit this description are not leaders —they are merely politicians.

Often even after people "sniff out" self-serving politicians and want to get rid of them, money from special groups keeps them in office year after year. In the end, this creates a sour taste in the mouths of voters, who wonder, "Why do we even vote? The people we elect seem to represent only the fringe of society. Is our vote really worth anything?"

We are in the midst of a great leadership crisis today. Husbands don't want to lead because they are afraid of offending or losing their wives. Fathers and mothers don't discipline their children because they're afraid of losing their children's affection or even of being accused of child abuse. Employers are afraid of being labeled racists if they don't hire an adequate number of minorities and, as a result, often pass up qualified job applicants in order to fill a predetermined quota of minority employees.

Schoolteachers don't want to take authority in their class-rooms because a student might claim that his or her rights are being violated. Instead of teaching kids that sex before marriage is a sin, teachers give condoms to high school students so they don't offend nonreligious organizations. Children now often have the right to "divorce" their parents if they don't like the way things are going at home.

Our nation's great leadership crisis is following the same pattern of decline and disintegration that existed in the Roman Empire prior to its collapse. The parallels are just amazing

Sadly, just as there is a leadership crisis in this nation's politi-cal arena, there is also a terrible, gaping hole in the leadership of the Church. Too often pastors struggle with asserting them-selves as God's chosen leaders in their churches. Some worry about whether or not their board of advisors will approve of their leadership style. Others worry about what will happen if they tell the worship leader to change the way he or she is leading worship. Still others worry about offending church members because they are afraid that people will leave the church and stop giving their tithes and offerings. Of course, this isn't true of every pastor, but it's true of far too many.

Whatever you fear will determine the decisions you make. If you fear the opinion of man, the fear of man will dictate your decisions. However, if you fear a holy God whom you know you will stand before one day, that holy fear will control the decisions you make.

In addition to other responsibilities, Denise and I are pastors of a large church in Moscow, Russia. Therefore, I understand the subtle fears that can nearly overtake you before you even realize you're under attack.

Moreover, as a Bible teacher who has gained some recognition, I know what it's like to teach a potentially unpopular message, and I'm very familiar with the paranoia that stems from a fear of man's opinion. I know what it's like to wonder if you'll be rejected for taking a stand that no one else wants to take or for teaching a message that isn't in agreement with what everyone else seems to be propagating at the time.

My own fear of man's opinion was blatantly exposed in my life many years ago after I wrote a book that challenged certain questionable practices that were emerging in a lot of churches at the time. Although many people were blessed by that book, I now believe that its primary purpose was for *my* benefit. Through that process, I became aware of a character flaw that desperately needed to change in order to move forward in my calling.

As that book rolled off the press, my telephone immediately began to ring. I received calls from ministers across the nation who said, "Please don't print that book. Let's just forget the off-balance doctrines that are being taught right now and walk in love with one another."

However, the reason I wrote that book in the first place was because I *was* walking in love! In God's eyes, the well-being of the Church is infinitely more important than how popular I am in man's eyes — and I am convinced that He was clearly leading me to take a stand that needed to be taken. Writing that book revealed a need in my life to submit my will and emotions to the power of God and to break the spirit of fear that was secretly trying to operate in my life.

This spirit of fear can be magnified exponentially in the life of a pastor who has to hear the constant murmurings, complaining, and opinions of his church members. As wonderful as the sheep of God are, there are times when they can really act like goats, kicking and butting in every direction!

It's remarkable that so many people who have an opinion or believe they've received a word from the Lord seem absolutely certain that their perspective is the only one that matters. This unwillingness to consider different points of view frequently causes turmoil in local churches. Even if a church has only 100 people in its congregation, it already has nearly 100 different opinions — and everyone is certain that his or her perspective is right. That means the pastor will inevitably offend someone when he makes a decision.

There is no way for a pastor to get around this particular challenge. That's why he should focus on doing what God has instructed him to do, realizing that he will never be able to please all the people under his charge. He can love them; he can listen to them — but in the end, he needs to stand up and lead them according to his best understanding of the Holy Spirit's direction.

When a leader never takes a strong stand nor gives clear direction to those under his charge, people can find it difficult and frustrating to follow him. On the other hand, people will support a strong leader, even if they don't always agree with his direction — because they respect his boldness and his courage to take a stand!

A Common Trait of Influential World Leaders

When I talk about a strong leader, I'm referring to a leader who displays strength of will — that ability to be focused, decisive, and resolute, regardless of external opposition or internal fears. Throughout history, we find numerous examples of people who willingly followed this type of strong-minded, determined leader.

- The children of Israel followed Moses out of 400 years of Egyptian slavery, even though the Red Sea loomed in front of them and Pharaoh's army was closing in from behind.

- Britain looked to Winston Churchill for leadership during World War II when the nation was facing the prospect of a sustained war and a possible invasion by Nazi Germany.

- Americans followed President Ronald Reagan's confident leadership as he implemented sweeping economic and political initiatives, helping to bring the nation out of a decade of national malaise and financial turmoil.

- The British people reelected Margaret Thatcher for three terms in the 1980s as she introduced policies that helped strengthen Britain's economy and stave off the nation's pattern of swift decline.

It's important to note that we can also find ample historical examples of strong leaders who, although evil in their ruthless pursuit of power, were still able to gather countless multitudes to themselves who readily followed them. Many of the leaders in this latter category were sadistic, power-hungry tyrants, obsessed with delusions of their own greatness and with no regard for the people who followed them. These leaders took their people in a very demonic and wicked direction — yet the people followed them anyway. What could possibly explain such a counter-productive choice? It was that one characteristic they shared in common with all the other historic leaders I mentioned above. Each of these leaders led with strength and confidence. This is a quality that people look for in a leader and to which they usually respond with total allegiance — even when that allegiance is directed toward an evil ruler and rooted in fear.

Where there is a vacuum of strong leadership, instability is the result. When that instability becomes rampant, no one wants to take a stand on any issue, and as a result, anarchy begins to spread throughout the nation. Eventually people become weary of this situation and want to return to a state where someone gives them purpose and direction. This is the perfect environment for terrible dictators to emerge, as was demonstrated in the 1930s when Hitler rose to a place of power in Germany.

However, it's also the golden moment for believers to hear God's voice and step forward to answer His call. The Church and the world are crying out for godly leadership right now.

Let me ask you this question: Have you ever visited a huge church where you had to search and search for a parking place before the service because there were so many members? But then as you sat through the service, did you sadly realize that it was one of the most boring church services you'd ever attended?

I've been to a few services like that. It's always an amazing thing to me to watch hundreds and even thousands of people rush to attend a service that is basically dead and uneventful. What's even more amazing to me is to see how committed the people are to faithfully attend each service and to give of their tithes and offerings.

> **The Church and the world are crying out for godly leadership right now.**

In such churches, the pastor speaks almost in a monotone voice, possessing no special preaching or teaching ability. The members look joyless as they hold their hymnbooks, and the choir stands on the platform like statues. By the time the altar call is finished, everyone attending is loaded with so much condemnation and bondage that they hardly crack a smile as they shuffle out the church doors.

On a few occasions, I've been invited to preach in churches like this. Often before I preach, I have the opportunity to sit in on an earlier service so I can experience the church and know exactly what kind of congregation I will be ministering to that night. If it's a church like I just described, I nearly always think to myself, *Why do all these people come here Sunday after Sunday? What motivates them to keep giving their tithes and offerings when they can't even smile at church? What is it about this church that attracts so many people to come here?"*

In many of these cases, the answer is the same — *the pastor is a strong leader.* He may not be the most exciting preacher by a long shot, but he is steady, strong, bold, courageous, and unwavering in his leadership style. There are no gray areas and no questionable issues about his lifestyle or behavior. He is exactly what people see — *strong, steady, and unwavering.*

People keep coming to these churches because the pastors have strong personalities that emanate strength to their congregations. Even though their preaching tends to put people to sleep, one thing is certain: These pastors are in charge, imparting their visions to their churches and requiring commitment of their members. No one doubts where these pastors stand or where they intend to lead their churches in the future. And because of their strong leadership, the people are able to follow them.

WEAK LEADERS
VS. STRONG LEADERS

Of course, this in no way minimizes the importance of a leader's responsibility to teach right doctrine to those under his charge. We are living in an hour when doctrine is being grossly ignored, which will ultimately prove to be spiritually fatal for many churches. But in addition to doctrine, people need to see strength in their leader. In fact, this is the main quality people look for in leadership. In Joshua 1:6, God commanded Joshua, "Be *strong*...." God knows that people aren't really looking for someone who is perfect and never makes a mistake; they want someone who can give them godly direction. *They want to see strength in their leader.*

This is the reason weak leaders eventually lose their businesses, congregations, or political offices. If a leader tends to waver on the decisions he makes and be easily influenced by special-interest groups, he will lose the respect of his followers, whether it's a congregation, a staff, or a nation.

> People aren't really looking for someone who is perfect and never makes a mistake; they want someone who can give them godly direction.

Be strong! Pray and discover God's plan for your life and your realm of influence, whether it's your family, your church, your business, your state, or your nation. Then make up your mind to do exactly what God puts in your heart. In His timing, make that announcement with faith, and then *hold fast* to that plan in faith. Establish your heart on what God has said, and never waver in front of the people He has put under your charge.

Even if you feel a little shaky on the inside about the decision you've made, keep that anxiety to yourself. You don't need to tell everything you think and feel to the people you're leading. If they see fear and instability in you, it will undermine your ability to lead. Don't tell them so much about what you're thinking and feeling that they cease to see you as a leader and begin to simply see you as a fellow struggler who is uncertain about what direction to take.

The people you're leading should see you standing strong even if you're feeling weak. If you have a need to tell someone that you're going through a struggle, talk to those who are closest to you and have seen you struggle in the past and emerge victorious. They will know how to encourage you.

Talk privately to your spouse, to your parents, to a faithful friend, or to your pastor. But don't spill your guts to your entire congregation or to all the people who work for you in your business, organization, or ministry. Instead, put a smile on your face and "fake" it!

Remember, your emotions are temporary, and it probably won't be long before your confidence and joy return to you as you continue walking in faith. If you were to prematurely talk about your temporary fears to the people under your leadership, they might remain affected by the anxiety you dumped on them long after your feelings of worry or fear dissipate and your faith takes over once again.

There is a time for you to keep your mouth shut and put on a happy face — even if you don't feel particularly happy.

If you are a leader, you don't have the privilege of showing the same kind of weakness that other people show. You can bare your heart to your closest friends and family if you must, but don't reveal your temporary doubts and fears to the people you're leading. Most of them simply wouldn't be able to handle it!

God continues to clarify this point to Joshua in verse 6 by saying, "...for unto this people shalt thou divide for an inheritance the land, which I sware unto their fathers to give them."

Notice that God says, "...for unto this people...." This phrase is very important because it reminds us that Joshua's new calling in life *connected him to people.*

Any leadership position God calls us to fill is always connected to people. A pastor without a congregation ceases to be a pastor. A husband without a wife ceases to be a husband. A parent without children ceases to be a parent. A president without a nation ceases to be a president.

Leadership is not derived from an official title, but from a relationship with people.

God wanted Joshua to understand this principle right from the start. So He said to His man, "Be strong and of a good courage: for unto this people...." If Joshua failed to give the children of Israel the strength and courage they needed in order to follow him over the Jordan River into the Promised Land, he would fail to be the leader God wanted him to be.

When God calls you to accept a new assignment that includes a leadership role, just as He did Joshua, it will require you to move into a new realm of faith, courage, and boldness. You probably won't feel prepared for it, but God has counted you faithful enough to handle it; otherwise, the door wouldn't have opened to you. *You can do it!*

A daily time of prayer and study in the Word of God is essential to fulfilling your new assignment, however. By constantly keeping yourself in remembrance of God's revealed plan for your life, you will project the strength and confidence people need to see in you. You can lead your people through all the challenges, difficulties, and problems — *right into the middle of their promised land!*

Turn Not to the Right or to the Left

In Joshua 1:7, God exhorted Joshua, "Only be thou strong and very courageous, that thou mayest observe to do according to all the law, which Moses my servant commanded thee: turn not from it to the right hand or to the left, that thou mayest prosper whithersoever thou goest."

What we find in verse 7 is that God desires careful obedience. He doesn't want you doing things your way when He gives you specific instructions for fulfilling His assignment; He wants you to do it exactly as He instructed you to do it.

For example, when God told Moses how to build the tabernacle, He gave Moses an intricate construction plan. I wonder if that tabernacle could be built today by a modern Church that is filled with so much sloppy obedience.

We need to make an unwavering commitment that we will not stray from the word God speaks to us. We will not turn to the right or the left but will do exactly what He directs us to do.

You'll have plenty of opportunities to "fudge" on a word from God, looking for shortcuts or an easier way to go about doing what He's asked you to do. And you may very well find another route that looks great — but if it isn't exactly what God said, don't you dare turn onto that path!

Be wary of people who say, "Do you really think that's what the Lord meant? You know you could interpret that two ways. I know what you *think* the Lord said, but let's consider *this*. We wouldn't be sensible if we refused to consider other options."

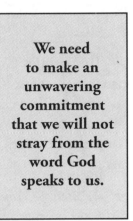

We need to make an unwavering commitment that we will not stray from the word God speaks to us.

I have heard these words so many times. But if you know in your heart that you've heard from God, you're foolish to consider other options or any other alternative to what God has spoken to you. Who in the world do we think we are to look for a better way than what He has commanded?

Notice what the Scripture goes on to say in verse 7: "...that thou mayest prosper whithersoever thou goest." When you do what God has asked you to do and you honor Him by doing it His way — seeking His perfect will in every aspect of it — you will prosper. *This is a Bible promise.*

This promise has been proven time and time again in my life. When Denise and I obeyed the Lord and moved our family to the Soviet Union, everything increased. Invitations to speak increased; our funds increased; the strength of our relationships with pastors and churches increased; and even our personal finances increased. Naturally speaking, this would have seemed impossible, but that is exactly what happened.

I don't even want to think about what we would have forfeited if Denise and I had not obeyed the Lord. But, thank God, we knew that if we obeyed Him and honored Him, we would ultimately experience the blessings that come with obedience to His will.

An Important Command

Three times God commanded Joshua to be strong and courageous. In verse 6, He told Joshua, "Be strong and of a good courage…." In verse 7, He said again, "Only be thou strong and very courageous…." And in verse 9, God repeated, "Have I not commanded thee? Be strong and of a good courage…."

Joshua must have been thinking, *Yes, yes, yes! I hear You, and I get the message! You want me to be strong and courageous!* But *why* did God keep repeating those words to him? *Because strength and courage are the most important elements of leadership.*

Notice that God didn't tell Joshua three times that he should pray or meditate or keep the vision in front of him. That doesn't mean those three things are not vitally important, but they're not the *most important* elements in leadership.

When God repeats a phrase, it's always for the sake of driving home a crucial point. So what is the first thing God requires of you? *Strength.* Whether He has called you to drive a school bus, be a college professor, run a company, or be a pastor, you will find that fulfilling God's will is difficult at times. The enemy does *not* want the Kingdom of God to advance. Satan is against you, and he will incite other people to be against you — sometimes even those who are dear to you.

There's a price to pay to serve God, no matter who you are or how high on the ladder of authority in your God-called realm you must ultimately climb. Therefore, you must be strong.

Remember, a leader is in relationship with the people he leads. Therefore, a true leader is someone who is always using his strength to encourage and build up others. And because of his inner strength, people are able to draw courage from him as they follow his lead.

Being strong and courageous doesn't mean that you promote yourself so everyone will know how anointed you are. It means you use your strength to encourage and lead your people. That's why God's command in Joshua 1:6, "Be strong and of a good courage...," is followed by the phrase, "...for unto this people...." Your strength and courage are *for the people*, because these qualities in you manifest as encouragement in those under your leadership.

You can pray, study the Word of God, and meditate on your God-given vision day and night. But if you don't consistently display true strength and courage and impart encouragement to those who follow you, you will fail as a leader.

After God had finished talking with Joshua, Joshua then turned to the officers of the people and gave them the Lord's instructions. As he stepped into his role as their leader, all the commanders came before Joshua and declared:

> **...All that thou commandest us we will do, and whithersoever thou sendest us, we will go. According as we hearkened unto Moses in all things, so will we hearken unto thee: only the Lord thy God be with thee, as he was with Moses. Whosoever he be that doth rebel against thy commandment, and will not hearken unto thy words in all that thou commandest him, he shall be put to death...."**
>
> **Joshua 1:16-18**

Most leaders would give anything for that kind of dedication! They look for people who will say, "Yes, we will do anything you ask us to do. We will go anywhere you tell us to go. We will hearken unto every word you speak to us. In fact, we are so committed to following you that if anyone in this church disobeys you and refuses to follow your commands, we'll eliminate them!"

That is loyalty and faithfulness of the highest, most sought-after magnitude! Can you imagine what Joshua must have been thinking at the moment? He probably thought, *Look at me! I'm quite a leader! My leadership ability is so strong that they will go wherever I tell them to go and do whatever I tell them to do.*

However, right in the midst of Joshua's inner exultation about how well things were going so far, his commanders ended their pledge with some familiar words: "...*only be strong and of a good courage*" (v. 18).

Now wait a minute! God already said that in verse 6, repeated it in verse 7, and spoke it again in an even stronger tone in verse 9. Now in verse 18, God said it again through the mouths of the people whom Joshua was called to lead! Joshua must have thought, *Were they listening when God spoke to me?*

Even the people knew that God had said to Joshua, "Be strong and of a good courage!" They were willing to follow and obey Joshua; all they wanted from him was clear, precise, strong, and courageous leadership. In other words, they were saying, "If you will really lead, then we will really follow."

As You Embark
on Your Next Assignment

As you strike out to tackle your next assignment in life, study the first chapter of Joshua and consider every point God spoke to Joshua's heart.

The waters before you may look dangerously wild and torrential. The people you're called to lead may bring problems and challenges, and the promised land God has set before you may be filled with conflict as well as blessing. However, if you step forward with courage, you'll enter into a new realm of miraculous living that you've never before experienced.

Pick up your feet, and take that first step into the unknown! That's where your faith will explode and the adventure will take off. You'll never know the joy of truly serving God in a life of faith by sitting at home, watching television, avoiding new challenges in life, and ignoring the voice of the Holy Spirit deep in your heart.

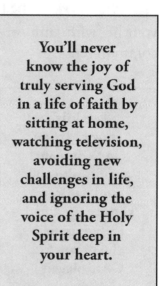

You'll never know the joy of truly serving God in a life of faith by sitting at home, watching television, avoiding new challenges in life, and ignoring the voice of the Holy Spirit deep in your heart.

Once the children of Israel hearkened unto the voice of Joshua and stepped into the Jordan River, God responded to their obedience with the miracle they needed to do the impossible: "...The priests that bare the ark of the covenant of the Lord stood firm on dry ground in the midst of Jordan, and all the Israelites passed over on dry ground, until all the people were passed clean over Jordan" (Joshua 3:17).

I am certain everyone shouted for joy when the waters parted and they passed over on dry ground. But no one rejoiced more than Joshua because this miracle was God's proof that Joshua was chosen to lead the nation of Israel during the next phase of His plan for them.

This miracle accomplished something else as well. It gave the people of Israel another dose of faith and encouragement, confirming that they were right on track. And just as they received encouragement in the wilderness by remembering the parting of the Red Sea, the memory of the parting of the Jordan River would sustain them when they reached the next crossroads of faith — their next point of no return.

So establish your heart on God's personal promises to you, and dedicate your entire life to bringing forth the dream He has placed within you. Tackle each new assignment in God's plan for your life with faith, strength, courage, confidence, boldness, and common sense.

> Establish your heart on God's personal promises to you, and dedicate your entire life to bringing forth the dream He has placed within you.

As you determine to do *all* that God requires of you in faith and obedience, I can promise you this: You will reach the point of no return many times over. But each time you forge through a new crossroads and step out in faith to fulfill the next assignment God has for you, you'll sense something working deep on the inside of you. There will be a new deposit of strength and courage to take on the unknown. You'll sense a greater expectation that God will help you do what seems impossible to man.

Thus, your journey in God will continue as you go "from glory to glory" (2 Corinthians 3:18). Then one day, you'll look back over your life and be able to say with strong confidence: "I followed Jesus through every *point of no return*. '…I have finished my course, I have kept the faith' (2 Timothy 4:7)!"

What a day of rejoicing that will be!

THINK ABOUT IT

You can't lead people if you're afraid of people. When a leader applies all his efforts to being politically correct in order to gain support or to court the affection of those he's appointed to lead, he nullifies his own potency, because the fear of man always brings a snare (Proverbs 29:25).

Are you faced with making a decision that you know is necessary yet unpopular? What emotions do you sense as you ponder the possibility of not pleasing people? When you consider the possibility of not pleasing God, what thoughts come to mind?

Be honest with yourself: Whom do you seek to please? Whose opinion do you value the most, God's or man's? You'll know which opinion matters the most to you by what you're willing to do or to endure in order to secure that one's approval. The one whose displeasure you fear is the one you will serve, and that allegiance brings its own consequence or reward: One costs and the other pays. Whom do you fear?

❧

Do you have a clear vision? Do you know where you're going and how to get there? Are you decisive and unwavering when a decision must be made? Are you direct when communicating your expectations, yet discreet when expressing your own qualms or concerns?

As you diligently cultivate these strong characteristics, you will inspire confidence and respect among those appointed to follow your lead. Most of all, you will be a worthy servant of the One whose leadership you both follow and represent.

REFERENCE BOOK LIST

1. How To Use New Testament Greek Study Aids by Walter Jerry Clark (Loizeaux Brothers).

2. Strong's Exhaustive Concordance of the Bible by James H. Strong.

3. The Interlinear Greek-English New Testament by George Ricker Berry (Baker Book House).

4. The Englishman's Greek Concordance of the New Testament by George Wigram (Hendrickson).

5. New Thayer's Greek-English Lexicon of the New Testament by Joseph Thayer (Hendrickson).

6. The Expanded Vine's Expository Dictionary of New Testament Words by W. E. Vine (Bethany).

7. Theological Dictionary of the New Testament by Geoffrey Bromiley; Gephard Kittle, ed. (Eerdmans).

8. The New Analytical Greek Lexicon; Wesley Perschbacher, ed. (Hendrickson).

9. The New Linguistic and Exegetical Key to the Greek New Testament by Cleon Rogers Jr. (Zondervan).

10. Word Studies in the Greek New Testament by Kenneth Wuest, 4 Volumes (Eerdmans).

11. New Testament Words by William Barclay (Westminster Press).

12. Word Meanings by Ralph Earle (Hendrickson).

13. International Critical Commentary Series; J. A. Emerton, C. E. B. Cranfield, and G. N. Stanton, eds. (T. & T. Clark International).

14. Vincent's Word Studies of the New Testament by Marvin R. Vincent, 4 Volumes (Hendrickson).

15. New International Dictionary of New Testament Theology; Verlyn D. Verbrugge, ed. (Zondervan).

Prayer of Salvation

When Jesus Christ comes into your life, you are immediately emancipated — totally set free from the bondage of sin!

If you have never received Jesus as your personal Savior, it is time to experience this new life for yourself! The first step to freedom is simple. Just pray this prayer from your heart:

Lord, I can never adequately thank You for all You did for me on the Cross. I am so undeserving, Jesus, but You came and gave Your life for me anyway. I repent and turn from my sins right now, Jesus. I receive You as my Savior, and I ask You to wash away my sin by Your precious blood. I thank You from the depths of my heart for doing what no one else could do for me. Had it not been for Your willingness to lay down Your life for me, I would be eternally lost.

Thank You, Jesus, that I am now redeemed by Your blood. You bore my sin, my sickness, my pain, my lack of peace, and my suffering on the Cross. Your blood has covered my sin, washed me whiter than snow, and given me rightstanding with the Father. I have no need to be ashamed of my past sins, because I am now a new creature in You. Old things have passed away, and all things have become new because I am in Jesus Christ (1 Corinthians 5:17).

Because of You, Jesus, today I am forgiven; I am filled with peace; and I am a joint heir with You! Satan no longer has a right to lay any claim on me. From a grateful heart, I will faithfully serve You the rest of my days!

If you prayed this prayer from your heart, something amazing has happened to you. No longer a servant to sin, you are now a servant of Almighty God. The evil spirits that once exacted every ounce of your being and required your all-inclusive servitude no longer possess the authorization to control you or to dictate your destiny.

If you prayed this prayer from your heart, something amazing has happened to you. No longer a servant to sin, you are now a servant of Almighty God. The evil spirits that once exacted every ounce of your being and required your all-inclusive servitude no longer possess the authorization to control you or to dictate your destiny.

As a result of your decision to turn your life over to Jesus Christ, your eternal home has been decided forever. HEAVEN is now your permanent address.

God's Spirit has moved into your own human spirit, and you have become the "temple of God" (1 Corinthians 6:19). What a miracle! To think that God, by His Spirit, now lives inside of you! I have never ceased to be amazed at this incredible miracle of God in my own life. He gave me (and you!) a new heart and then made us His home!

Now you have a new Lord and Master, and His name is Jesus. From this moment on, the Spirit of God will work in you and supernaturally energize you to fulfill God's will for your life. Everything will change for you now — and it's all going to change for the best!

If you prayed this prayer for the first time, please call or email
our Renner Ministries office.
We would love to pray with you!

Phone: 918-496-3213
Email: **prayer@renner.org**.

ABOUT THE AUTHOR

Rick Renner is a respected leader and teacher within the Christian community, both in the U.S. and abroad. He fills a unique position in the modern Christian world, combining an extraordinary depth of scriptural and practical knowledge with an easy-to-understand, faith-filled approach to the Bible. Rick became passionate about the Greek New Testament when studying Journalism and Classical Greek as a university student. In the years that followed, he continued his extensive study of the Greek New Testament, later earning a Doctor of Philosophy in Ministry.

Along with his wife Denise and their sons and families, Rick works to see the Gospel preached, leadership trained, and churches established throughout the world. Together, their global mission is to teach, strengthen, and rescue. Rick is the founder of the *Good News Television Network* (aka *Media Mir*), the first Christian television network established in the former Soviet Union that today broadcasts the Gospel to a potential audience of 110 million people. His broadcast "Good News With Rick Renner" can be seen across the entire former USSR. Rick has distributed hundreds of thousands of teaching audio and videotapes, and his best-selling books have been translated into four major languages. In addition, Rick teaches via the Internet with English-speaking broadcasts.

Rick is the founder of the *"It's Possible"* humanitarian foundation, an organization committed to providing for the practical needs of various segments of Russian society. He is also the founder of the *Good News Association of Pastors and Churches,* through which he oversees and strengthens hundreds of churches throughout the former Soviet Union. In addition, Rick and Denise pastor the thriving *Moscow Good News Church*, located in the very heart of Moscow, Russia. *RENNER Ministries* has offices in Russia, Ukraine, Latvia, England, and the United States. Rick resides in Moscow with his wife and their three sons and families.

ABOUT OUR WORK
IN THE FORMER USSR

From inception to its current role in the Body of Christ, *RENNER Ministries*' purpose and vision has been to teach, strengthen, and rescue people for the Kingdom of God. Although the Renners' ministry began much earlier, in 1991 God called Rick and Denise Renner and their family to what is now the former Soviet Union. Since that time, millions of lives have been touched by the various outreaches of *RENNER Ministries*. Nevertheless, the Renners' ever-increasing vision for this region of the world continues to expand across 11 time zones to reach 300 million precious souls for God's Kingdom.

The *Moscow Good News Church* was begun in September 2000 in the very heart of Moscow, right next to Red Square. Since that time, the church has grown to become one of the largest Protestant churches in Moscow and a strategic model for pastors throughout this region of the world to learn from and emulate. Today the outreaches of the *Moscow Good News Church* includes ministry to families, senior citizens, children, youth, and international church members, as well as a specialized ministry to businesspeople and an outreach to the poor and needy. Rick and Denise also founded churches in Riga, Latvia, and in Kiev, Ukraine, both of which continue to thrive.

Part of the mission of *RENNER Ministries* is to come alongside pastors and ministers and take them to a higher level of excellence and professionalism in the ministry. Therefore, since 1991 when the walls of Communism first collapsed, this ministry has been working in the former USSR to train and equip pastors, church leaders, and ministers, helping them attain the necessary skills and knowledge to fulfill the ministries that the Lord has given to them.

To this end, Rick Renner founded both a seminary and a ministerial association. The *Good News Seminary* is a school that operates as a part of the *Moscow Good News Church*. It specializes in training leaders to start new churches all over the former Soviet Union. The *Good News Association of Pastors and Churches* is a church-planting and church-supporting organization with a membership of pastors and churches that numbers in the hundreds.

RENNER Ministries also owns and operates the *Good News Television Network*, the first and one of the largest TV outreaches within the territory of the former USSR. Since its inception in 1992, this television network has become one of the strongest instruments available today for declaring the Word of God to the 15 nations of the former Soviet Union, reaching 110 million potential viewers every day with the Gospel of Jesus Christ.

In addition, Rick Renner also founded the *"It's Possible!"* humanitarian foundation, which is involved in various outreaches in the city of Moscow. The *"It's Possible"* foundation uses innovative methods to help different age groups of people who are in great need.

If you would like to learn more about our work in the former Soviet Union, please visit our website at www.renner.org, or call 918-496-3213.

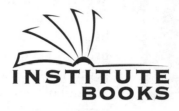

INSTITUTE BOOKS, INC.

Teaching you can trust.

A Division of Renner Institute, Inc.

8316 E. 73rd St., Suite 207

Tulsa, OK 74133

Phone: 918-893-3433

Fax: 918-893-2444

Email: contact@rennerinstitute.com

A LIGHT IN DARKNESS
VOLUME ONE

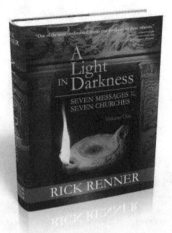

Step into the world of the First Century Church as Rick Renner creates a panoramic experience of unsurpassed detail to transport you into the ancient lands of the seven churches of Asia Minor. Within the context of this fascinating — and, at times, shocking — historical backdrop, Rick outlines challenges early believers faced in taking the Gospel to a pagan world. After presenting a riveting account of the apostle John's vision of the exalted Christ, Rick leads you through an in-depth study of Jesus' messages to the churches of Ephesus and Smyrna — profoundly relevant messages that still resonate for His Church today.

$79.95 (Hardback)
ISBN 978-0-9779459-8-6

Rick's richly detailed historical narrative, enhanced by classic artwork and superb photographs shot on location at archeological sites, will make the lands and the message of the Bible come alive to you as never before. Parallels between Roman society of the First Century and the modern world prove the current relevance of Christ's warning and instructions.

A Light in Darkness is an extraordinary book series that will endure and speak to generations to come. This authoritative first volume is a virtual encyclopedia of knowledge — a definitive *go-to* resource for any student of the Bible and a classic *must-have* for Christian families everywhere.

Faced with daunting challenges, the modern Church *must* give urgent heed to what the Holy Spirit is saying in order to be equipped for the end of this age.

For more information, visit us online at: **www.renner.org**
Book Resellers: Contact Harrison House at 800-888-4126,
or visit **www.harrisonhouse.com** for quantity discounts.

MINING THE TREASURES
OF GOD'S WORD

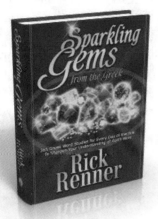

Author Rick Renner unearths a rich treasure trove of truths in his remarkable devotional, **Sparkling Gems From the Greek.** Drawing from an extensive study of both the Bible and New Testament Greek, Rick illuminates 365 passages with more than 1,285 in-depth Greek word studies. Far from intellectualizing, he blends his solid instruction with practical applications and refreshing insights. Find challenge, reassurance, comfort, and reminders of God's abiding love and healing every day of the year.

$34.95 (Hardback)
ISBN: 978-0-9725454-2-6

Sparkling Gems From the Greek Electronic Reference Edition

Now you are only a few short clicks away from discovering the untold riches of God's Word! Offering embedded links to three exhaustive indices for ultimate ease in cross-referencing scriptures and Greek word studies, this unique computer study tool gives you both convenience and portability as you read and explore Rick Renner's one-of-a-kind daily devotional!

$29.95 (CD-ROM)
ISBN: 978-0-9725454-7-1

A BIBLICAL APPROACH
TO SPIRITUAL WARFARE

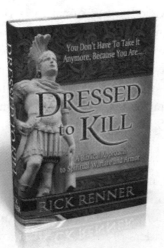

Rick Renner's book *Dressed To Kill* is considered by many to be a true classic on the subject of scriptural warfare. The original version, which sold more than 400,000 copies, is a curriculum staple in Bible schools worldwide. In this beautifully bound hardback volume, you will find:

- 512 pages of reedited text

- 16 pages of full-color illustrations

- Questions at the end of each chapter to guide you into deeper study

$24.95 (Hardback)
ISBN: 978-0-9779459-0-0

In *Dressed To Kill*, Rick explains with exacting detail the purpose and function of each piece of Roman armor. In the process, he describes the significance of our *spiritual* armor not only to withstand the onslaughts of the enemy and but also to overturn the tendencies of the carnal mind. Furthermore, Rick delivers a clear, scriptural presentation on the biblical definition of spiritual warfare — what it is and what it is not.

When you walk with God in deliberate, continual fellowship, He will enrobe you with Himself. Armed with the knowledge of who you are in Him, you will be dressed and dangerous to the works of darkness, unflinching in the face of conflict, and fully equipped to take the offensive and gain mastery over any opposition from your spiritual foe. You don't have to accept defeat anymore once you are *dressed to kill!*

For more information, visit us online at: **www.renner.org**
Book Resellers: Contact Harrison House at 800-888-4126,
or visit **www.harrisonhouse.com** for quantity discounts.

BOOKS BY RICK RENNER

*Digital version available for Kindle, Nook, iBook, and other eBook formats.

Note: For audio and video teaching materials by Rick Renner,
please visit **www.renner.org**

Books in Russian

Dream Thieves

Dressed To Kill

The Dynamic Duo

Good News About Your New Life

If You Were God, Would You Choose You?

Insights to Successful Leadership

Isn't It Time for You To Get Over It?

Hell Is a Real Place

How To Test Spiritual Manifestations

A Light in Darkness, Volume One

Living in the Combat Zone

Merchandising the Anointing

Paid in Full

The Point of No Return

Seducing Spirits and Doctrines of Demons

Sparkling Gems From the Greek Daily Devotional

Spiritual Weapons To Defeat the Enemy

Ten Guidelines To Help You Achieve
  Your Long-Awaited Promotion!

365 Days of Power

What the Bible Says About Healing

What the Bible Says About Tithes and Offerings

What the Bible Says About Water Baptism

What To Do if You've Had a Failure

The Harrison House Vision

Proclaiming the truth and the power

Of the Gospel of Jesus Christ

With excellence;

Challenging Christians to

Live victoriously,

Grow spiritually,

Know God intimately.